A pocket guide to investing in

Positive Cash Flow Property

MARGARET LOMAS

Wrightbooks

First published Febuary 2004 by Wrightbooks.
an imprint of John Wiley & Sons Australia, Ltd
33 Park Road, Milton, Qld 4064

Offices also in Sydney and Melbourne

Typeset in Else LT Light 11/13.5 pt

© Margaret Lomas 2004

Reprinted October 2004

National Library of Australia
Cataloguing-in-Publication data:

Lomas, Margaret.

A pocket guide to investing in positive cash flow property.

Includes index.
ISBN 0 7314 0113 1.

1. Real estate investment. I. Title.

332.6324

All rights reserved. No part of this publication may be reproduced, stored in a retrieval system, or transmitted in any form or by any means, electronic, mechanical, photocopying, recording, or otherwise, without the prior permission of the publisher.

Cover design Rob Cowpe

Printed in Australia by Griffin Press

10 9 8 7 6 5 4 3 2

Disclaimer

The material in this publication is of the nature of general comment only, and neither purports nor intends to be advice. Readers should not act on the basis of any matter in this publication without considering (and if appropriate taking) professional advice with due regard to their own particular circumstances. The author and publisher expressly disclaim all and any liability to any person, whether a purchaser of this publication or not, in respect of anything and of the consequences of anything done or omitted to be done by any such person in reliance, whether in whole or part, upon the whole or any part of the contents of this publication.

Contents

	Preface	ix
Step 1:	Your Current Capacity to Invest	1
Step 2:	Start Your Search	27
Step 3:	Doing the Research	63
Step 4:	Making Your Choice and Signing Contracts	87
Step 5:	Applying for Finance	111
Step 6:	The Conveyancing Process	141
Step 7:	Property Management	153
Step 8:	Preparing for Tax	173
Step 9:	Selling Your Property	199
Step 10:	A Few Extra Insights	215
	Note from the Author	221
	Glossary	223
	Index	231

Dedication

As always, my husband Reuben has given me the support, guidance and encouragement I have needed to write this book, despite the tough times which 2003 brought to us. I thank you for that and for everything else you have given me.

Suellen, a lifelong friend – thank you for your support this past year and always.

Dad – one year on and I still miss you every minute. Not having you to read my work has left a big hole. I hope you are watching – this book is for you.

FREE SOFTWARE!

Congratulations on your purchase. You are now entitled to download your free copy of Destiny Finsoft, a unique program only available to readers of Margaret's books.

The program includes:

- Buying and selling worksheets
- Loan calculators
- Property cash flow calculators
- Depreciation calculators
- Purchase and loan stamp duty calculators
- Finance qualifier
- Ready to invest calculator.

Just about everything you need to assist you with the important tasks you are about to undertake.

To download this software, you will need to first email download@edestiny.com.au and provide your name and contact details. You will receive a password within a few days. Then, go to:

www.edestiny.com.au/finsoftentry.html

Enter the barcode and this new password, and you will receive complete instructions about how to download this wonderful program.

Enjoy using it!

Acknowledgments

Teresa – you know that I cannot run my life or business without you! Thank you for everything.

Steve and Dave from the 2GO real estate show – I love you guys, and you constantly support and encourage me. It's such fun working with you, and I look forward to great things in our future.

Susan and Juliette – commitment and desire are concepts you do not need explained to you. You are both very special to me.

Mark – the enthusiasm you continue to show will remain your biggest asset. Head down and tail up and you will amaze yourself with what you achieve. How proud I am that you are my son.

Noel Whittaker – how privileged I am to be able to call you friend and mentor. Thanks for being in my life and for the wonderful guidance you give.

Kristy, Belinda, Michael and Rebecca – I must be the luckiest mother in the world to have such great children – you are all independent, strong and verbal! I cannot wait to see your lives unfold and am so glad I can be a part of that. Thank you for your patience and, most of all, your unconditional love.

Karyn, Chris, Mark and Paul – my brothers and sister. Well, you all had to put up with me, didn't you? That in itself bears acknowledging – thank you!

And last but not least, to the special radio people who are always so good to me – Tony Delroy (ABC), Annette Allison (3AK), Graeme Maybury (6PR) Laurie and Paula (Bay FM breakfast). Talking to you is always fantastic and your support is remarkable.

Don't worry if I missed you this time – books keep walking out of my head so I'll get you next time. It doesn't mean you are not important to me – it just means that the world is so full of wonderful people, I would need another book simply to thank them all!

Preface

A few months ago a reader called and told me about his successes with buying positive cash flow property. He had previously purchased a series of properties that were negative cash flow and, since being alerted to the concepts of positive cash flow through my books, he had managed to turn his negative cash flow around.

He said that all of the books in my 'How to' series had been of great use, but to make things easier for himself he had spent countless hours extracting the information he needed to put together a systematic process – a step-by-step guide. This ensured that he could easily get on with the business of seeking out and buying the right kind of property without the worry that he might overlook any crucial steps.

It was then I realised that when I buy property for myself I do so largely using an unconscious series of steps which feel innate to me. Of course they are – not only is buying property my hobby and my investment of choice, it is also my job. I have the benefit of being able to eat, sleep and think about property for most of my waking hours. I am so involved in property that the process of property investing is second nature to me now.

However, most of my readers are not so lucky. They spend their lives working on other things – either in a job for someone else, in a business for themselves or perhaps caring for a family. They do not have the benefit of being immersed in the property industry so constantly and, therefore, buying property can seem like an arduous and cumbersome task.

My 'How to' series of property books covers every single aspect of buying property and includes everything you could ever wish to know about buying and managing positive cash flow property – from the moment you decide that property is for you, right through to the day you settle on a property and beyond. Be sure to read them first, and keep them handy as many references are made to them in this book to allow you to gain more comprehensive information about each phase of the investing process. However, there is a lot of information to digest, and while it is crucial that these books are read if you want to gain an in-depth knowledge of

Preface

property investing, it can be time consuming to go back and sift through each of these books time and time again to uncover and formulate an actual process which you can use.

With this in mind, a new book idea began to germinate within my head until it became an absolute consuming need to put pen to paper and make your job of buying property a whole lot easier. This book will not replace any of my previous property books – they will remain vital pre-reading if you are ever to have a complete understanding of positive cash flow property and so achieve ultimate success when you do invest.

However, once you have read the concepts detailed in my other books, *A Pocket Guide to Investing in Positive Cash Flow Property* will provide you with a step-by-step process to taking action. It will take much of the hard work out of the job of investing and ensure that you miss nothing when buying a property. Keep the book with you at all times, follow the references to my other books to gain a more in-depth understanding, and then follow every step outlined in this guide and you will be sure to maximise your chances of buying a well-performing property that will help you to meet your financial goals for years to come. It will keep you from getting caught up with the emotions of buying property and help to ensure that you truly use a commercial head when making choices. It will allow you to use that vital 'financial advising' approach which I so strongly encourage all investors to adopt when seeking suitable property, and this will steer you clear of the inherent pitfalls of dealing with most property marketers today.

Although this pocket guide is concerned mostly with walking you through the buying process, I have added some information on selling towards the end of the book, to ensure you can exit your investment in the best possible financial shape.

When you know you are doing something well, you can also enjoy what you are doing. As a stress reduction tool, this little book may be the key to providing enough peace of mind for you to enjoy and make the most of your property investing. It provides a pathway that leaves little to chance and much to good management and clever buying.

Hope you enjoy it!

Margaret Lomas
January, 2004

Step 1

Your Current Capacity to Invest

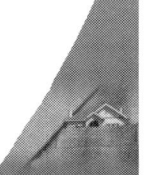

Before you go away on a holiday you will normally have some sort of plan in place. Usually, you will know your destination, have planned a budget and packed the required items you feel you will need when you are away. You may even pack in a few 'contingency' items such as warmer clothes in the event of bad weather, or an extra credit card in the unlikely event that you overspend!

When people buy property as an investment many of them spend far less time on this task than they do on planning their holiday. For some, the opportunity to invest may arise while they're actually on a holiday, and they will return home the proud owners of a fancy new apartment by the beach.

For others a Sunday drive will lead straight to a real estate agent's office where a slick talking salesman convinces them quite quickly that his latest listing is just the investment property they need.

A property investment involves decisions that are not to be taken lightly. Like all major life events, commencing or continuing a property investment portfolio requires education, thought and a large degree of planning. To put this plan into action you must start by understanding exactly what it is you will be looking for, and assessing your own capacity to purchase. Over-committing yourself can have dire consequences, but under-committing yourself may also mean you are not utilising opportunities which are available to you.

> **Tip!** Start your planning by photocopying the relevant worksheets and checklists from the end of each section of this book – do one set for each property you are looking at. This way you will be sure not to miss any steps. Then start a 'Property Portfolio File' in which you can keep all of your documents and worksheets.

If this is the first book you have read on buying positive cash flow property, then you need to go back and get hold of some of my previous 'How to' books. *How to Create an Income for Life* gives a very detailed explanation of exactly what positive cash flow property is all about. Many people who think they understand this concept are rather surprised at how complex it really is, and at how many different opportunities for positive cash flow investing there are in Australia.

I won't try to explain the entire concept again from scratch but, in a nutshell, here are the three main ways that you can invest in property today.

1. Negative gearing

Quite simply this is where you buy a property (with borrowed funds) which has more expenses than income, and you lose money, week after week. This loss can be partially offset by some of your income tax being returned to you, but there is still some money required from your pocket to make up the shortfall.

For example:

Property price:	$150,000
Income:	$9,500 per annum
Expenses:	$9,500 interest
	$3,000 other
Loss:	$3,000 per annum
Tax back at 30%:	$900
True loss:	$2,100 or $40 per week

This would be a typical result for most properties bought in capital cities at the time of writing. Why? Because most of our capital cities have had, or are having, a property boom.

Although a property may boom in price, the rent return usually remains stable, or rises only according to the consumer price index (CPI). Even if purchase prices subsequently plateau, it could take many years before the rent returns will have risen enough to close the gap between income and expenses which the boom has caused, and bring a property back to a point where the return becomes enough to once again cover the ongoing costs.

Why do people buy properties that are going to take money out of their pockets, week in, week out? Usually because they believe that, at some time in the foreseeable future the property value will rise so much that this weekly cost will be justified and they will be able to make up all their losses and earn a profit with a large gain made upon sale.

They may also rationalise that their losses are tax deductible and so they are actually being 'smart' and paying less tax.

> **Tip:** Buying a negative cash flow property just to reduce your tax is like spending a dollar to save 47 cents.

Of course the problems here are many, including the fact that the number of properties you can buy with a weekly loss is limited to the amount of disposable income you have, and if you are constantly losing money you may not be able to build up a buffer to manage risks such as rising interest rates and higher than expected vacancy rates. (See 'Hedging and Leveraging with Positive Cash Flow Property' on page 65 of *How to Create an Income for Life* for more information on managing the risks of investing in property.)

> **Short-term investors are more likely to choose negative cash flow as they want quick gains and can afford to pay money from their own pockets over the short term required to achieve this (provided they have managed to secure growth properties).**

2. Positive gearing

As the name would suggest, this is the opposite of negative gearing, and occurs where you have been lucky enough to find a property with a higher than average rent return for the purchase price, and/or the expenses (other than loan interest) are lower than average. Of course you will pay income tax on any gain this creates.

For example:

Property price:	$150,000
Rental income:	$14,000 per annum
Expenses:	$9,500 interest
	$2,000 other
Gain:	$2,500 per annum
Tax paid at 30%:	$750
True gain:	$1,750 or $34 per week

Properties such as this are usually found in large regional centres, industrial towns or country areas. This is because wages in Australia are relatively stable across the country and the cost of renting is linked to the consumer price index, which ultimately determines wages. The trade off for this higher return is often thought to be a slower growth in prices, and hence, a lower capital gain. However, this is not necessarily proving to be correct in recent times, with many investors seeing excellent growth rates where they have been careful in selecting regional areas that satisfy a range of criteria (covered in Step 3 of this book). On the downside, this has meant that it is becoming increasingly difficult to find a suitable regional area or country town which has yet to 'take off'.

3. Positive cash flow

In fact, positive cash flow is still known to the tax department as negative gearing, as you are 'gearing' the property (that is, using borrowed money to buy it) and experiencing a 'loss'. I like to use this term, however, as it describes the type of negatively geared property which actually gives you money in your pocket each week. This is because the loss on this kind of property is on paper only.

> **Tip!** Long-term investors will be more likely to choose positively geared or positive cash flow property as this way the property not only pays for itself, but has time in which to deliver a capital gain as well.

Positive cash flow is where you buy the kind of property which qualifies for on-paper deductions. That is, it is built within the allowable period for you to 'set off' a range of items, such as the original costs of construction and the assessed value of the fixtures, fittings and furniture against any income you make from the property and from your employment. The best thing about these kinds of deductions (explored in depth in later sections) is that you can claim them for many years without having to pay anything out. These claims result in tax refunds which, in turn, give you the additional cash you may need to pay those expenses not covered by rental income.

> **Tip!** Be aware that on-paper deductions, such as asset depreciation, eventually run out. The combined effect, however, of increased rent return and attention to serious debt reduction by you will ensure that the property still makes a positive cash flow even after you have claimed your limit in deductions.

For example:

Property price:	$150,000
Rental income:	$9,500 per annum
Expenses:	$9,500 interest
	$3,000 other
On-paper claims:	$9,000
Claimed loss:	$12,000 per annum
Tax back: (30% on loss of $12,000):	$3,600

True gain:
$9,500 rent + $3,600 tax back − $12,500 costs
= $600 ($11.55 per week)

Property such as this is far more abundant than positively geared property because any property built after 1985 carries allowable deductions. However, just because a property was built within the allowable timeframe will not make it positive cash flow – this depends not only on the amount of on-paper deductions a particular property will allow you, but also on the rent return and your own marginal rate of tax.

> **Tip!** If you have a higher marginal rate of tax, the amount you pay – and hence the amount you can save – in tax payments will be greater and you will have more choices available.

As you buy more and more property, you will find you have lots of deductions to claim and, since you only pay so much in tax, the amount you are entitled to have returned is limited. When you've reached your limit it will become necessary for you to seek out more 'positively geared property' for a while, as this will then provide you with additional taxable income, against which more deductions can be written off.

Where to start

Once you have decided to start or to continue a property portfolio, it helps to know a little more about what you are capable of achieving before you begin. This will ensure you avoid instances where you find exactly the right kind of property, but discover that you are unable to buy it because you are not yet in a position to do so, or the bank will not lend to you. I also find many situations where people come to me for advice, and discover they could have commenced investing many years ago, but did not realise this.

Since positive cash flow property puts dollars in your pocket each week, even after you have paid out all of the required expenses, it may seem that this means you should be able to buy as many properties as you like. Sadly, if you are borrowing to invest, the banks don't quite see it this way. Most banks are more inclined to focus on your commitment to repay their loans rather than the actual 'cash in your pocket' benefits such properties can provide.

The formulas we are about to discuss will assist you to determine what you can achieve and to establish whether a bank will provide the necessary funds for you to start investing.

> **Tip!** One of the best things about choosing positive cash flow property is that it gives you extra money each week that you can apply towards rapid debt reduction. Debt reduction equals more equity, which equals faster property acquisition.

Your position

You must start by deciding how much equity you would like to maintain across your entire portfolio. By this I mean, how much do you want to own, and how much do you want the bank to own.

When I first began investing, I felt that keeping 20% ownership across my entire portfolio would provide me with a suitable buffer in the unlikely event that I had to sell up.

If my estimations were wildly wrong and interest rates skyrocketed to the point where all of my properties had to be liquidated, I felt that, with 20% ownership, I had a good chance of coming out of the portfolio in the same position I went in.

Some people like to take more or less risk than this. If you are a risk-taker, you may wish to keep only 10% ownership. This would mean that, in the first few years your position may be a bit precarious, but it will improve over time as the values of your properties grow.

It would also mean that you would have to pay out additional costs in the form of lender's mortgage insurance on your investment loans, which means that your properties would have to perform a little better to recover this additional cost. Alternatively, you may be more conservative and wish to own more of your property – perhaps 30%, or even 40%.

> **Tip!** Be sure you are clear about how much equity you would like to retain before you start, and stick to that. This will ensure your personal need for safety is always maintained

The choice is yours alone – no-one else can make this decision for you. Do not allow property marketers or people with no formal financial advising qualifications to talk you into making a purchase which is outside of your comfort zone. Not only will you worry endlessly about your investment, but you will never forgive yourself if it does fail. I do encourage you, however, not to wait until you own your own home outright before you invest at all. This is wasting time and will not substantially reduce the risk factor anyway. If you are worried that you will lose everything and have yet to read *How to Create an Income or Life*, do so now as there is an entire section (page 3) devoted to analysing the true risks of investing which should put this into perspective for you.

> **Tip!** Use the free Destiny Finsoft 'Ready to Invest' calculator (download instructions on page 236) to establish your equity and borrowing capacity.

How many can I buy?

All through this book we will be talking about buying property using a loan for the entire cost of that property. You will not be required to bring in any cash of your own unless you own no property at all, or have no equity available in the property you do own. Where you have equity in existing property, this becomes your 'deposit' so to speak, as equity in property is virtually the same as money in the bank.

You should know the price range in which you feel most comfortable. A client of mine some years ago had a real desire to invest but simply could not bring herself to do so. She came very close several times, but reneged each time the contracts appeared. After examining this with her, I was able to determine that it was the *price* of the potential investments that worried her – $200,000 seemed a lot to borrow (she had no personal debt and owned her own home), so when we looked at properties under $100,000 (yes, they do still exist) she felt far more comfortable. That was less than two years ago and she now has a total loan portfolio of more than $600,000 on five properties. Better still she is growing more and more confident every day and is actively seeking to add to this portfolio all the time.

> **Tip!** There are a few unique organisations – such as my own company, Destiny Financial Solutions – which can prepare an analysis for you based on your personal circumstances and provide you with a 10- or 15-year property acquisition strategy.

Once you have determined a price range with which you are comfortable, use the following steps to determine how many properties you may be able to buy now. Note that this is the formula for a person wishing to keep 20% ownership. If you have a different requirement, substitute the percentage of equity (first step) with the figure you are prepared to mortgage.

1. Total property values today x 80% = total borrowing capacity on security
2. Total borrowing capacity – total current securitised debt = deposit funds available
3. Deposit available less an amount for purchasing (say $10,000) = 20% of new property
4. 20% of new property x 5 = potential purchase price or maximum spend.

Illustration:

Stella and Jack have $300,000 worth of property with a debt of $180,000.

1. $300,000 x 80% = $240,000 (borrowing capacity)
2. $240,000 – 180,000 = $60,000 (deposit funds available)

cont'd...

Illustration *(cont'd):*

3. $60,000 − $10,000 = $50,000 (20% of new property)

4. $50,000 × 5 = $250,000 (maximum price of new property)

Stella and Jack can spend up to $250,000 on a new property and still retain at least 20% ownership across both properties. If they did spend this amount, their new position would be as shown in Figure 1.1, below.

Figure 1.1
Stella and Jack's Position

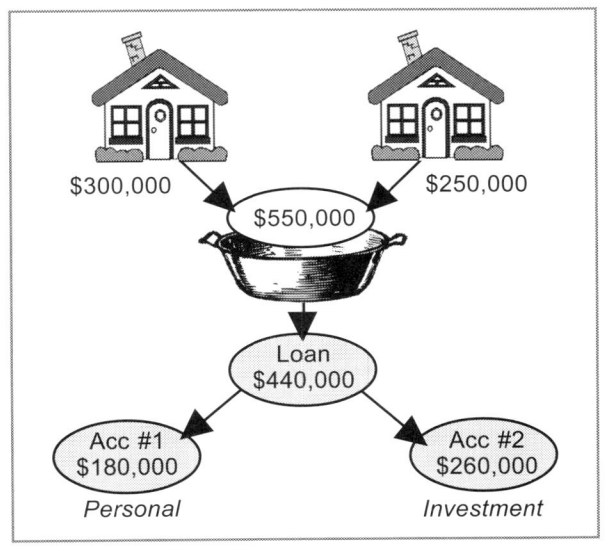

> **Tip!** A lender will usually advance up to 80% of purchase price or valuation, whichever is the lower. Buying 'below valuation' does not necessarily mean that you can borrow more.

Of course, where there is more equity than this, and the capacity exists to purchase more than one property, then more than one lot of purchasing costs must be taken into account. This formula is a basic guide only which helps to establish a ballpark figure for your new purchase or an idea of the number of properties you may be able to buy. Be sure to be as conservative as possible when estimating the current values of properties you own. You may have an idea of what you think a property is worth, but usually the bank's valuer will not agree, and it will be the valuer's estimation that determines how much you can borrow, not yours. In later sections we will look at exactly how a bank values a property, and this should assist you.

> **Tip!** If you want to know what your property is really worth, check out the recent sales in the area for similar properties – this will be more accurate than a real estate agent's opinion.

It is vital that, as you build your portfolio, you redo this calculation, preferably every 12 months. This is because the values should rise steadily over time and if you have bought positive cash flow property you should also be gaining equity in your debt at the same time. It was two years between my first and second property purchases and last year I bought three in the one week. The more you add to your portfolio, the more exposure to growth you will have, and the quicker you will be able to buy additional properties.

> **Tip!** I like to allow an additional safety margin which can then cover unexpected costs in the early years. In addition to the purchasing costs, you might like to allow an extra $2,000 to $3,000 for costs on each property you purchase. Interest on any loan funds used to pay costs is tax deductible, as are the costs themselves.

What will the bank let me do?

Of course, you may have a substantial amount of equity in current property, and the formula above may show that you can rush out tomorrow and buy $2 million worth of investment property and still retain a good amount of equity, but what will the bank say when you breeze in with an application for a $2 million loan?

These days there are an abundance of books and seminars designed to help you become a property millionaire at the speed of light. While some of these courses and books are based on strategies which sound good in theory, many ignore the basic facts – banks are quite conservative and they could just provide a bit of a stumbling block for you.

> **Tip!** Be extremely careful of any information coming from an expensive workshop. In the history of investing anything sounding too good to be true always has been and this still applies today. Check the ASIC website (www.asic.gov.au) for warnings before considering any upcoming workshop or scheme.

True, there are many lenders around which provide a range of flexible loan options and each has different lending criteria, but if you are like me you may well want to stay with the more well-known lenders to ensure that you are not paying premium rates for funds from lenders with uncertain backing.

While each bank or non-bank lender has different lending criteria, you can ascertain a ballpark figure of your borrowing capacity using a basic formula known as a debt servicing ratio.

You can also ring around and have the banks give you a ballpark figure for your borrowing capacity. In addition, some banks now have an online conditional approval process, where you can get approval for a loan amount (subject to a range of criteria) and even print off a certificate of approval.

Debt servicing ratio (DSR)

A DSR relates to your capacity to repay a debt. It has nothing to do with your equity position, although a bank will approve a loan only if you can satisfy both its income criteria *and* its equity criteria. I have had many potential clients ask me why a bank will not lend to them when they have tonnes of equity, but no income, and many other clients wondering why the bank will not lend to them when they have extremely high incomes but no assets. Put simply, banks want to be sure that, firstly, you will be able to apply your income to the job of debt repayment (and if you have a high income and no assets, this may indicate an inability to save) and, secondly, that you have enough equity to cover any shortfall in what you owe them in the event that you are forced to sell up.

As a rule of thumb, most lending institutions today will allow you to commit up to 35% of your gross income to debt commitments. In other words you can borrow an amount of money which requires no more than 35% of your gross income, as a monthly figure, to repay. When this calculation is done, all loans are taken into account – so if you already have personal loans or credit cards, the commitment to these should also be included in the calculations.

Let's look at an example:

> **Illustration:**
>
> Stephanie and Shane have a credit card with a limit of $5,000, and a personal loan with a repayment of $500 a month. They wish to borrow $120,000 for a property. They have an income of $50,000 per annum and will see $10,000 per annum in rental income from this new property.
>
> Using 35% as a debt servicing ratio, this means that the bank would allow them to commit $20,300 to loan repayments, as they would consider all of the $50,000 as well as 80% of the rental income of $10,000 ($50,000 + $8,000 x 35% = $20,300). Will they be allowed to borrow $120,000?
>
> So far they have committed $1,800 per annum to the credit card, assuming 3% of the $5,000 limit as a monthly repayment ($5,000 x 3% x 12 = $1,800) and $6,000 to the personal loan ($4,500 x 12 = $6,000). This makes a total of $7,800, which leaves them with $12,500 of allowable income to use for loan repayments.
>
> The required repayment to finalise this new loan in a 25-year period would be $861.19 per month (assuming a 7.17% interest rate), which equates to $10,334 per annum. So, providing that they meet the rest of the bank's criteria, they would probably have their loan approved.
>
> *cont'd...*

> **Illustration (cont'd):**
>
> The formula for calculating whether you would qualify for a loan using a DSR is:
>
> $$DSR = \frac{(\text{Annual loan repayments} + \text{All other debt commitments}) \times 100}{\text{Total income} + 80\% \text{ rent}}$$
>
> The result must be less than 35% to qualify for a loan.

Lenders will use a higher than current interest rate as an 'approval rate' when calculating your serviceability. In this example, I have used the current approval rate at the time of writing, which was 7.17%. They will also assume a principal and interest repayment to perform the calculations, even if the loan you are seeking is an interest-only loan or a line of credit.

Most lenders have a standard list of income types they will accept when calculating your serviceability for a loan. Some banks also allow the interest portion of any debt being used for investing to be 'added back', so to speak. This means they are accepting that it is a tax deduction to you and, in effect, that this tax deduction increases your available income.

If you think that your bank will 'add back' the loan interest, decrease the required loan repayments by the amount of this interest when using the above formula.

> **Consulting a financial adviser who specialises in property investment will mean that all of these permutations, and more, can be taken into account for you.**

It is important to note that many banks use what are known as 'serviceability criteria' rather than a DSR. These criteria involve a complicated formula that takes into account all commitments, including family expenses, to arrive at a borrowing capacity. This method is outlined in more depth in *How to Create an Income for Life* (page 137), and the free software available to readers, Destiny Finsoft, can do an approximate serviceability calculation for you.

Regardless of the method your bank uses, the DSR formula we have discussed should at least indicate a ballpark figure and help you to know if you are close to the required income for the loan you are seeking.

> **Use the loan repayment calculator in Destiny Finsoft to establish the monthly P&I repayment for the potential loan you are seeking.**

Worksheet 1.1:
How Many Properties Can You Buy?

1. Total current property values $..............

Multiplied by

2. 80% = Total borrowing capacity $..............

Less

3. Your current debt $..............

Equals

4. The deposit available $..............

Less

5. Purchasing costs
   (say $10,000 each property) $..............

Equals

6. 20% of new property(s) $..............

Multiplied by

7. Five (if using 80%) $..............

(purchase price/total available spend)

Worksheet 1.2:
Calculating Your Debt Servicing Ratio (DSR)

1. Your existing loan repayments $............

Plus

2. Potential new loan repayments $............

Equals

3. Total loan repayments $............ (A)

Multiply by

4. 100 $............ (B)

5. Total gross income
   (inc. 80% rent) $............ (C)

6. Divide B by C $............ (%)

If the result is less than 35% you may qualify for this new debt.

☑ *Step 1 Checklist*

☐ Ascertain whether you want to buy positive cash flow property or negative cash flow property. To do this, ask yourself the following questions:

　i. Do I have excess disposable income which I am prepared to spend on a property?

　ii. How much excess do I have? If I am looking at, say, three or four purchases, do I have the excess funds to support three or four negatively geared properties?

　iii. If not, am I prepared for the fact that positively geared property and positive cash flow property may grow at a slower rate than negatively geared property?

　iv. What is my timeframe for investing? If short-term you may be prepared to fund a loss, and if long-term you will want property which pays for itself.

☐ Decide how much equity you wish to maintain across your portfolio. I recommend at least 20% but you may have a different need.

☐ Calculate how many properties you can afford according to your current equity. Use Worksheet 1.1 on page 23 to determine this. Make sure you redo these calculations each year as the values increase.

☑ *Step 1 Checklist (cont'd)*

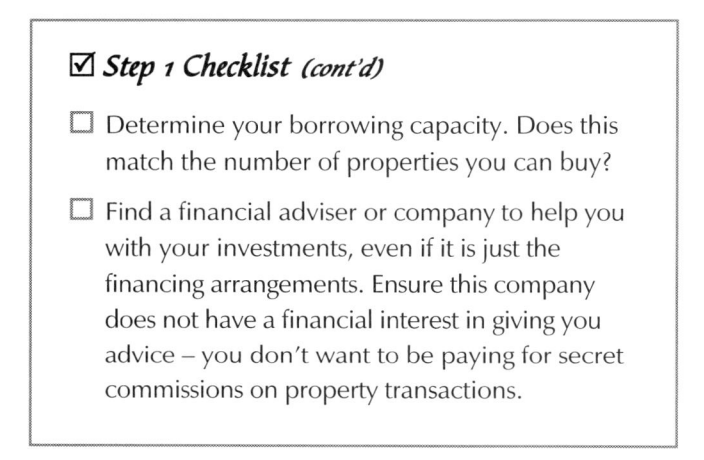

☐ Determine your borrowing capacity. Does this match the number of properties you can buy?

☐ Find a financial adviser or company to help you with your investments, even if it is just the financing arrangements. Ensure this company does not have a financial interest in giving you advice – you don't want to be paying for secret commissions on property transactions.

Step 2

Start Your Search

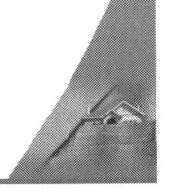

The question I probably encounter most of all is "Where do you find positive cash flow property?" If I had the magic formula, then I would use it myself every day. Just because positive cash flow property provides a relatively secure, financially viable investment does not mean that you can sit back and hope that it appears out of thin air for you! On the contrary, there is much work to be done both in the search for, and the research of, positive cash flow property.

What I *can* say is that, once you have bought a few properties, it does become easier. You begin to know how to recognise the right kind of property before you put in too much hard work. You start to know instinctively the types of areas that may have positive cash flow property, and so you search them out. As you become more experienced you can tell far sooner if a property is simply not going to stack up.

> **Tip!** In time, recognising the right property will become a subconscious process.

Meanwhile, you have to begin your search and my experience is that most people limit themselves by not casting the net far enough – in doing so they miss viable opportunities. There are many places to seek out property, and you should not think that your local real estate agent is your only option.

> **Tip!** The best investment property for you may be in another state altogether.

Where to buy

Often, when buying property as an investment, something happens to previously intelligent people and they lose much of their reasoning power. This phenomenon can generally be put down to emotions getting in the way of good sense.

Usually, people who decide they want to buy a property as an investment will start locally. Since they have chosen the area to live in, it must be a good area, don't you agree?

When it comes to good areas, 'good' means different things in an investment property context than it does when choosing a place to live for you and your family. Granted, tenants may seek out similar things to you when it comes to choosing a property in which to reside, but the realities are that most tenants are rather itinerant. They may be between owner occupied properties, moving about with work or otherwise inclined to stay for a relatively short time, so many long-term features you seek out in a home of your own simply will not appeal to them.

> **Tip!** 'Good' for an investment property means tenant friendly, basic design, close to amenities such as public transport, close to shopping centres, appropriate for the demographic group of the area (e.g. where population is aged, ground floor accommodation will be imperative, etc), and in a price range which makes it easy to sell in the event that you need to.

Even so, investors tend to cast the net five kilometres around where they live, and this is where they choose to invest. "I'd like to keep an eye on it", they tell me when I ask why they need to have the investment so close by.

Quite frankly, the last thing I want is to be able to actually watch my investment, to see how the tenants are *not* looking after my property, or to be in any way involved in its management. This might be a nice idea if you have one or two properties, but if you are serious about a property portfolio then, once you have three or more, the reality is that you simply cannot become so involved.

Positive cash flow property exists all over Australia, and the very property which is most right for you may be in another state altogether. To ignore this fact is to miss out on some fantastic opportunities for both cash flow and growth in a property.

> **Tip!** When you think about buying a property, treat it just like any other asset class. When you buy a share, you will research it but won't necessarily visit the company's head office or meet its staff. The same principle MUST apply to your property purchasing – you must become commercial and focus on the facts and figures, not on your feelings and emotions.

In the next step, we will explore the questions you must ask to ensure that you can safely buy property which you do not necessarily visit to inspect. For now, let's look at all of the possible sources you can use to find a positive cash flow property.

1. The internet

The internet is a rich source of property information, and the best thing is that you can do your research at midnight wearing pyjamas and hair curlers if you so desire! Advances in technology have made it possible for you to perform virtual tours, and these are almost as good as visiting a property yourself.

Certainly when using the internet to find property the only things which you cannot get a good feel for are features such as the actual structural soundness of the property or its comparative value to other properties in the area. Since you are probably not qualified to make these judgements anyway, this is a job to leave to the experts once you have narrowed down the choices.

Start with a general search using the Google website (www.google.com.au). At the search prompt, type in 'properties under' and the dollar value you have determined from Step 1 to be your comfort zone and within your price range. This is going to return an abundance of pages, so begin by clicking on them one by one.

Next, go to real estate specific websites. These include sites such as www.property.com.au and www.realestate.com.au, as well as those sites which belong to real estate chains. All of them will offer a search page where you can specify your search criteria and narrow down the pages you will have to look through. These sites are a little more specific than Google, although you can search an entire state rather than a particular area if you do not have an area in mind yet.

> **Tip!** Clever photography can make any property look great – you can be just as prone to an emotional attachment on the internet as you can be when you go to look in person. Don't be swayed by fantastic pictures as they may not be telling the true story. Nothing can replace your research.

2. Newspapers

Of course, your local newspaper will list many of the available properties in your area, but did you know that many newspapers, including those of the Community Newspaper Group, have their classified advertisements available on the internet?

The websites of local newspapers can be a great place to seek out property in any area, and will also provide a good chance for you to look at comparative values and expected rent returns once you have some properties on your list.

3. Register as a user

Many of the larger real estate company sites will offer you the opportunity to register with them and specify your needs. By providing some basic contact details such as your own email address, you can specify your requirements in terms of price, property type, size and area. Then, every time a new listing satisfying your criteria becomes available, the details are automatically sent to you.

Even when you are not actually in the market for property, this can be a great way to stay in touch, keep up with values and monitor your own portfolio.

4. Property clubs, etc.

While these can be a great way to find property, do be very careful. There is an abundance of property and investor clubs that you can join, but almost all of them have a premium built into the price of any properties they list. Often this will be considerably more than standard real estate institute recommendations, and can be as much as an additional 10%. Even those clubs claiming to be 'non-profit' rarely are, and the notion that they are a group of interested investors simply trying to provide a community service is one which is cleverly fostered by astute marketers.

By all means register with these people (if it is free) but research each group thoroughly to find out what is in it for them. It is reasonable for a property club or an internet-based property provider to include standard real estate commissions paid to them by the vendor (as would any real estate agent) and, if they perform a greater service (such as providing marketing services for the developer) they may charge the developer a small additional fee which comes from developer profit, not from your pocket. Your thorough, independent research of the market should help you to gain a deeper understanding of the true values in the areas you are seeking, so you should know if the available properties are fairly priced.

> **Tip!** The fact that your friends or dozens of other people are registered with a particular club does not automatically make it legitimate. It can be very easy to be influenced by others and to want to become part of a wave of people who seem to know what they are doing. Use common sense and ask a good number of questions before becoming involved and always be suspicious if there is a cost.

5. *Expos and trade shows*

Expos and trade shows provide a wonderful opportunity for you to obtain lots of information in a short period of time. In addition, these days, most shows will also feature a host of expert guests and keynote speakers so, for a small entry fee, you are able to gain some good education.

Do be careful though. Little model buildings proudly displaying future developments cost tens of thousands – sometimes up to $100,000 – to produce. Where does this money come from? It can be so easy to be caught up with the excitement and not realise that all of the information given to you by the enthusiastic presenters at such expos is simply marketing hype. Rarely do stated returns ever materialise, and they are extremely subjective anyway. Although the misleading and deceptive conduct provisions of the Trade Practices Act do apply, there is little else in the form of consumer protection to guard against the activities of over-zealous developers' agents.

Never sign anything on the spot. Use any information gained from an expo to simply add to your list of possibilities – and then carry out the same amount of due diligence as you would on a property which came to you with no marketing material whatsoever.

> **Tip!** **To find out about expos in your area, try these websites:**
> www.ausexhibit.com.au
> www.moneyexpo.ninemsn.com.au
> www.perthmoneyshow.com
> www.adlex.com.au

6. Developer direct

Properties may come to you directly from a developer in a number of ways. You may be telemarketed to and offered a 'free investment seminar', a developer's agent may visit you in your home, you may hear an advertisement on the radio or see one in a newspaper, or you may be lucky (or unlucky) enough to be the subject of a targeted campaign where you are whisked off to the Gold Coast and entertained vigorously until you sign on the dotted line.

It is possible that you'll find a great property in this manner but, all too often, it will be at a price which is way above true market value. Although two-tiered marketing (the practice of having one price for locals and another for interstate buyers) is now illegal in Queensland, this doesn't mean it does not still happen. Good quality, positive cash flow property will sell itself and does not need the frills and the flashy marketing campaigns.

> **Tip!** If a developer is selling his property far outside of his state, it may be because the locals know something you don't.

7. Auctions

I am including auctions in the list, not as a viable place to find a great property, but as a warning. If you want the full picture on auctions, be sure to grab one of Neil Jenman's books which all include a full discussion of the subject (see www.jenman.com.au).

Auctions often do not provide the opportunity for you to do enough research, and in most cases they result in a contract which cannot be rescinded, even in the event that you find undesirable features in the property you have bought. However, more importantly, even if you can do enough research and reassure yourself that the cash flow may be positive, auctions are usually an invitation to become emotional and to pay more than you intended, or worse, far too much to make a positive cash flow possible.

In the event that you must go to an auction, and you have done all of your research beforehand, be sure you are aware of the top price you can pay to still get a positive cash flow and stick to it.

8. Your local real estate agent

If you are one of the lucky people who live in an area which also has positive cash flow rental property available, then by all means go along to your local real estate agent and see what it has to offer. However, do remember what real estate agents do for a living – they are skilled and qualified to sell you the physical aspects of any property but they cannot give you financial or investment advice. They cannot know if the property in question is right for your personal circumstances, and very few real estate agents are aware of, or even understand, the true concept of positive cash flow property. So, don't have expectations they cannot fulfil, and don't ask questions which you know it is in their best interests to answer with whatever they think you want to hear.

> **Tip!** Only ever ask real estate agents questions about the physicality of a property. Do not ask about investment potential or even about rent returns as they simply do not know the answers to these questions.

9. Buyers' advocates

Buyers' advocates are people or organisations that will act on your behalf to seek out property based on criteria you provide. Usually their services will be related to the area in which they operate, although some of them will travel about the state or even interstate if they have enough clients to service. This can be a very good way of getting exactly the property you want without having to put in too much effort yourself, but be aware that they can be costly. Sometimes they will charge as much as 10% to 12% of the ultimate purchase price, and it is unlikely that they will carry out the type of exhaustive research you really need. Few of these organisations seem to fully understand the concept of positive cash flow property.

Start Your Search

> **Tip!** The fee for a buyer's advocate is considered an expense and the bank will not lend this amount to you unless you have the equity in property to support this extra borrowing.

What next?

After using these resources and finding a number of properties in different locations that may suit you, note down the names of the suburbs or areas of any properties not within a capital city or regional centre that you are familiar with. Then perform another internet search on this location to find out as much as you can about it. Set some benchmarks for yourself in terms of population and demographics. I always ensure that the areas I begin to research have a population of more than 20,000 and are not based around one industry alone.

> **Tip!** Just because a property listed by a real estate agent carries the byline 'Great Investment' does not mean it really is.

Most local councils have some kind of website so you should be able to get some useful information about any unfamiliar localities in this way. In addition, each state has a Real Estate Institute website, and some of these websites have great information such as vacancy rates for different areas, mean prices, local purchasing information, etc. The website addresses are:

- www.reiact.com.au
- www.reisa.com.au
- www.reinsw.com.au
- www.reit.com.au
- www.reint.com.au
- www.reiv.com.au
- www.reiq.com.au
- www.reiwa.com.au

Once you have a list of properties in your price range, visit a number of real estate websites and do a rental property search. You are doing this to glean potential figures for rent returns, which you can then use in your basic estimates to ensure you have a good chance of the properties being positive cash flow before you spend too much time on them. Simply indicate the suburb or area in which the property you have found exists as your search criteria and you should have a list of possible vacant properties returned to you.

As an alternative, telephone a local property manager (not the real estate company listing the property) and pretend you are seeking to rent a property which has the characteristics of the ones you are looking at. If there are no listings, this means one of two things – the area is very small and few people rent (which is a bad thing), or there are few available rentals at present (which is a good thing).

Start Your Search

If there are an abundance of listings this may mean that there is an oversupply or no demand for that type of property. Under these circumstances, you must investigate the reasons by carrying out more detailed research (see Step 3), or omit that property from your list. Remember though, that any estimates you make at this point are very subjective and are only done to weed out those properties with no real chance of showing positive cash flow.

From this action you should be able to narrow down a shortlist of properties which seem like they satisfy your criteria for positive cash flow, and you will be ready to carry out the research phase. Remember to keep anything you have found in your Property Portfolio File.

Some quick calculations

Of course, using all of the avenues discussed may well result in a list so long that by the time you have sifted through it property prices will have risen by 20%! You may just find that many of the properties on your shortlist end up being negative cash flow anyway, so you will have wasted time.

How to Maximise Your Property Portfolio included a ready reckoner table which allowed readers to do a quick estimate on the cash flow of any property they were considering. This information reappears in Table 2.1 at the end of this section. It gives sample depreciation amounts for particular types of properties in different price ranges, with special notes for their use.

Once you have used this table and adjusted it for the property you have found, you may wish to email download@edestiny.com.au and download the free Destiny Finsoft software. It has a range of wonderful calculation tools, including a cash flow calculator. If you like things to be simple, like I do, you will find this calculator far more user-friendly than some of the varieties available at a cost on the market today, as it provides you with a simple bottom-line figure representing your weekly and yearly cash flow amounts.

I personally find it rather difficult to interpret some software programs which have lots of complicated 'after tax' and 'before tax' figures expressed as a percentage return. At the end of the day you only need to know if there will be money in your pocket or not.

> **Tip!** Contact a large, well-known quantity surveyor like **www.depreciator.com.au** and ask if it can send you a sample depreciation schedule. You can then use this as a guide to the possible on-paper deductions which you may find in the properties you are looking at.

However, you may not carry your computer around with you, and in the event that you cannot get to your calculator and would like to know some quick cash flow figures, I also use one of two quick methods of calculation in the first instance. The first one gives me an actual amount of possible cash flow. The second one merely illustrates if the purchase price is at a level which will allow me to break even or get a positive cash flow.

Method #1

❶ (Purchase price + $10,000 (Purchasing costs)) × Interest rate = Interest costs

❷ Interest costs + $2,000 = Yearly actual costs

❸ Yearly rent − Yearly actual costs − Depreciation = Loss

❹ Loss × Marginal rate of tax = Tax back

❺ Rent + Tax back − Yearly actual costs = Cash flow

The year one depreciation amounts I use for this very quick calculation are usually as follows:

New house: $3,000 building, $4,000 year one fixtures and fittings.

New unit: $1,500 building, $5,000 fixtures and fittings (higher for common items).

Older house: $2,000 building, $3,000 year one fixtures and fittings.

Older unit: $1,000 building, $4,000 fixtures fittings.

Use your common sense here. Of course, if you are buying a property for $75,000, then you are not going to have $2,000 in building depreciation, since building depreciation is 2.5% of the original construction price and does not include any land component. A new apartment with state-of-the-art fixtures and fittings, a pool, gymnasium and lift will have far more fixtures and fittings depreciation than I have listed above.

Where a property is outside the allowable period for on-paper deductions (see Step 8) then the raw rent return must simply exceed the expenses as there will be no deductions allowed.

Method #2

As a rule of thumb we assume that for every 0.25% that the rent return is below the interest rate, you will need $320 worth of on-paper tax deductions for each $100,000 in price plus a further $2,000 in on-paper deductions to cover your base costs (assumed at $2,000) to make up the shortfall (if you are in the highest marginal rate of tax).

Start Your Search

The following example shows how this method works in practice:

Price:	$150,000
Interest rate:	6% or $9,000
Rent return:	5% or $7,500
Costs:	$2,000

Rent return is 1% below interest rate, so on-paper deductions must be equivalent to $1,920 ($320 for each 0.25% of $100,000 since the price is $150,000) plus $2,000 to cover base costs. In the example above, the bottom line would then be:

❶ $7,500 − $9,000 − $2,000 = − $3,500
(Rent) (Interest) (Costs) (True loss)

❷ $3,500 + $3,920 = $7,420
           (Deductions)   (Claimable losses)

❸ $7,420 x 47% (Tax rate*) = $3,487 (Tax back)

❹ $7,500 + $3,487 − $11,000 = $93
(Rent) (Tax back) (Total costs) (Virtually breakeven)

* This must be adjusted for different marginal rates of tax.

From this example you can see that if you can get, say, a 6% rent return, then you will only need to have $2,000 in on-paper deductions to get enough tax back to make up the shortfall. If the rent return was 7% you would have a loss of $500 (after interest and base costs) and so would need $500 of on-paper deductions to make up this shortfall.

At a 6% interest rate, the breakeven point (where no on-paper deductions are required) will be somewhere around 8% rent return, depending on the costs of the property (which will be greater if strata titled).

> **Tip!** A strata titled property may have more on-paper deductions due to the ability to offset your share of common property, but it will also have more costs due to strata levies.

Note that you can allow a margin for error or unforeseen costs with both of these formulas by using a higher interest rate or a lower rent return. This can then determine how low you can go in terms of return or how high you can go in terms of interest rate and still maintain your positive cash flow. Do always remember that these are very subjective figures based on your estimations and you may be very wrong. If the resulting cash flow from using one of these formulae is very tight, be aware that the end result may be a negative cash flow if you have underestimated expenses or overestimated on-paper deductions.

Property types and risk factors

Just as share investors choose a share based on their aversion to risk, and managed fund investors choose a managed fund with underlying assets matching their personal risk profiles, property investors need to be aware that different types of property carry different levels of risk.

All too often investors have asked me why I do not invest in more commercial property when it clearly has a higher return rate (being around 10% to 11% in most cases). I have to explain that this higher return comes at a price, in the form of higher risk.

> **Tip!** When choosing the type of investment you will buy, consider both your risk tolerance and disposable income. Just because you may have a high amount of disposable dollars does not necessarily mean that you also embrace risk.

How to Make Your Money Last as Long as You Do (Chapter 7) and *How to Create an Income for Life* (Chapter 3) take a comprehensive look at different property types and their risk profiles. Here is a summary.

Residential property

- Standard houses or units which are residentially tenanted
- Freehold, strata titled, community titled, torrens titled
- Fully tax deductible with on-paper deductions if built after 1985
- Capital gains tax applies on sale at a discounted rate if held 12 months or more
- Subject to demand which is linked to success of the area.

Risks

- If vacant you bear the costs alone
- Tenants may cause damage and flee
- You may buy in an area which becomes less popular over time
- Property is generally illiquid
- Diversity is less possible than with shares or managed funds due to the size of investments.

Conclusion: Suits investors with a low tolerance to risk and lower disposable income.

> **Tip!** The newer the property the higher the on-paper deductions, and the lower the maintenance costs.

Commercial property

- Factories, shops, offices, warehouses
- Freehold, strata titled, torrens titled
- Tax deductible if built after 1992
- May have business deductions if bought for own business
- Higher return than residential so can be highly positive cash flow
- Capital gains tax applies with no discount although there is a provision to roll over commercial premises which are part of an investor's own business into a pension structure.

Risks

- Vacancy can be more frequent and for longer periods of time
- Landlords usually have to offer incentives such as rent-free periods and help with fit-out to attract tenants from what is often a small pool
- In addition to the risk of vacancy there is the commercial risk – if the economy falters and their businesses go broke, your tenants may be unable to see out their leases.

Conclusion: Suits investors with a high tolerance to risk and a lower disposable income.

Vacant land

- Only has capital growth potential
- Capital gain will be taxed at the rate applicable to its purpose
- No tax deductions available until it becomes income producing
- Little or no ongoing costs except the interest on the loan.

Risks

- No major risks except that you must fund any debt on your own and hope the gain covers what you have paid out.

Conclusion: Suits investors with low tolerance to risk and high disposable income.

Holiday apartments, serviced apartments, hotels and resorts

- Income producing only in holiday periods
- Strata titled, freehold, community titled and torrens titled
- Rent returns can be more equal to commercial property
- Can be a range of management structures including on-site care-taking or management by a large hotel group

- Lifestyle benefits can apply if investor also uses property for personal use.

Risks

- Manager has complete control over success or failure of business
- Expenses can blowout if poorly managed, eating into profits
- The area you buy in may go out of fashion
- Lifestyle benefits may create a tax problem as the tax department considers these to be a form of 'soft dollar' income
- Income can be seasonally affected
- If the original purpose for the property fails (for example, you have a tourism property that no-one frequents) you need to be sure that you can let it as a standard residential property. Be sure that council zoning does not preclude this change of use.

Conclusion: Suits investors with medium to high tolerance to risk and medium levels of disposable income.

Choosing the right type for you

Choosing the right type of property for you to buy involves two major steps.

Firstly, you must be sure you completely understand your personal risk profile by completing the risk analysis questionnaire in Worksheet 2.3 at the end of this section. This will help to ensure that you can sleep at night because you will buy the type of property that most suits your own risk profile.

Secondly, you must then understand that successful property purchasing involves knowing enough about your market, and the existing demand, to be sure you buy a property which suits the demographic group in that area.

For example, there is no point buying a state-of-the-art, very up-market apartment on the 26th floor designed for young married people with no children if the demographics of the area dictate that residents are largely young families or retired people.

This research phase of your property acquisition is most vital – know your market and so ensure that you buy the product with the highest chance of success. More about the types of questions to ask about a potential property can be found in Step 3.

> **Tip!** Doing all the research and buying on figures and facts rather than emotions will ensure that you get a good investment and help you to satisfy your need for safety.

Worksheet 2.1: Cash Flow Calculation #1

1. Purchase price + $10,000	$..............
Multiplied by	
2. Interest rate	..............%
Equals	
3. Interest costs	$..............
4. Interest costs + $2,000	$.............. (Yearly actual costs)
5. Yearly rent	$..............
Less	
6. Yearly actual costs	$..............
Less	
7. Depreciation	$..............
Equals	
8. Loss	$..............
9. Loss x marginal rate of tax	$.............. (tax back)
10. Yearly rent	$..............
Plus	
11. Tax back	$..............
Less	
12. Yearly actual costs	$..............
Equals	
13 Annual cash flow	$..............

Worksheet 2.2:
Cash Flow Calculation #2

1. Purchase price + $10,000 $..............

Multiplied by

1. Price $..............

2. Rent return $..............

3. Rent return as a percentage of price (yearly rent/price x 100) ....%

4. Interest rate ....%

5. Difference between return rate and interest rate ....%

6. Divided by 0.25% ....

7. Multiplied by $320 for every $100,000 $..............

8. Add $2,000 (same amount as costs) $..............
   Rent return 5% or

9. Equals minimum on-paper deductions required $..............

Worksheet 2.3:
Your Risk Profile

The following questions will help you to identify your risk profile. Pick one answer in each section.

How would you describe yourself?

1. Retired and dependent on existing funds and/or pensions for income.
2. At the peak of your career and income, possibly with a dual income. You have no dependants or easily manage the expense needs of your dependants.
3. With a family to support. While you understand the need to invest, you cannot see how it will be possible, as your income is fully committed to the family budget.
4. Easily managing your current financial commitments. Your current income provides an acceptable lifestyle. You may be just starting out on your career or be well-established.

What is your understanding of investing?

1. Not very familiar with it.
2. You understand the need to diversify but no more.
3. You understand how different markets produce differing income and growth, and therefore have differing taxation implications.
4. You are an experienced investor with a current portfolio.

cont'd...

Worksheet 2.3 (cont'd): Your Risk Profile

What are your financial goals?

1. Income from an investment is the most important thing to you.
2. Safety is the most important feature for you.
3. You have a specific timeframe of, say, around five years and a set return you would like to achieve in that time.
4. Growth is the most important thing to you.

If your investments were to lose value by 25%, what would your reaction be?

1. Shock that your security of capital is affected.
2. You would decide to transfer what was left to something safer.
3. You would be concerned but would wait and see for a while.
4. You would not be concerned – you might even invest more while you can get a bargain!

Which do you prefer?

1. Guaranteed returns.
2. Consistent returns with minimal tax savings.
3. Variable returns with good tax savings.
4. Higher returns with maximum tax savings (but higher risk).

cont'd...

Worksheet 2.3 (cont'd): Your Risk Profile

When do you plan to retire?
1. Already retired.
2. Within five years.
3. In 5 to 15 years.
4. In more than 15 years.

How often do you switch your investments?
1. Whenever you have a loss.
2. Every three years at the most.
3. Every three to five years.
4. Every five years or more.

Use the Following Formula to Add Up Your Score

For every 1 answer, score one point.

For every 2 answer, score two points.

For every 3 answer, score three points.

For every 4 answer, score four points.

cont'd...

Worksheet 2.3 (cont'd): Your Risk Profile

Your Results:

0–7 points: Conservative

Preserving your capital is the most important consideration for you. You have a short-term investment period in which income and capital stability is of prime concern. You should invest in cash and fixed interest, and avoid shares and offshore investments.

8–12 points: Stable

Your investment term is three to five years, and you are willing to take a small degree of short-term instability if it means the chance of long-term returns. Security is very important to you, and income is more important than growth. Diversified funds and a good spread across all classes are most recommended for you, with a slight emphasis on property and fixed interest.

13–17 points: Moderately Balanced

You have a relatively long period in which to invest and are comfortable with short-term volatility for long-term growth and income. That is, you would like some security but are prepared to take a small amount of risk. You should look for investments which provide a balance of income and growth, and could also try some offshore investments with exposure to exchange rate risks.

cont'd...

Worksheet 2.3 (cont'd): Your Risk Profile

18–21 points: Balanced

Capital growth over a longer investment term is important to you. You should choose diverse investments. Equities, property and international investments should feature strongly in your portfolio, balanced by some cash and fixed interest. While income is required, your focus is on growth.

22–25 points: Growth/Assertive

You look for growth investments and are willing to include some speculative investments. You can cope with negative returns and increased volatility. Capital growth is your prime concern. You should invest mainly in sharemarkets, balanced with property. You have little need for fixed-interest or cash investments.

26–28 points: Aggressive

You can take volatility and will pursue higher long-term returns. You accept and expect negative returns at times in exchange for these long-term high returns. Maximum growth is your aim, and your most likely investment is domestic and international shares with little else.

Table 2.1
Sample Depreciation Figures with Notes

Building Type	Purchase Price ($)	Year 1 Depreciation ($)	Year 1–5 Total Depr. ($)
1 BR Unit	300,000	8,000	38,000
2 BR Unit	400,000	10,000	45,000
3 BR Unit	450,000	12,000	55,000
Townhouse	300,000	6,000	25,000
Townhouse	400,000	7,000	30,000
Residential	250,000	5,500	24,000
Residential	375,000	6,500	28,000
Commercial	2.5 mill.	100,000	450,000
Industrial	1 mill.	35,000	165,000

Reproduced here with the permission of BMT and Assoc. Quantity Surveyors.

Margaret's tips for using this table:

- The depreciation benefits obtainable depend greatly on the type of building, its age, use and fitout. Based on diminishing value depreciation, the above scenarios are provided as an appropriate guide.
- Depreciation in year one can be up to 30% to 40% of the total depreciation depending on the method used and the amount of first year 100% write-offs.

Start Your Search

- For properties which are not new, deduct 5% of the total year one depreciation, making it (for a one year old property) 5% of $5,500 for year one, then 5% of $5,225 for year two, then 5% of $4,963 for year three etc.
- For properties with prices outside of the above, make the necessary adjustments to the depreciation.

☑ *Step 2 Checklist*

- ☐ Risk profile performed
- ☐ Types of properties most suitable identified
- ☐ Google.com search performed
- ☐ Real estate websites checked
- ☐ Property.com.au and realestate.com.au checked
- ☐ Registered with websites specifying search criteria
- ☐ Australia-wide newspaper search completed
- ☐ Local real estate agency scanned
- ☐ Buyer's advocate sought if required
- ☐ Areas researched through local councils and the internet
- ☐ Local stats obtained including demographic mix
- ☐ Basic cash flow calculations performed

Step 3

Doing the Research

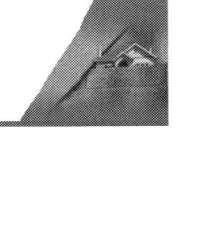

When they make the decision to buy a new car, most people go to great lengths to be sure that they buy the car most suited to their needs. Often this involves visits to many different car dealers, copious test drives, comparisons of facts, figures and opinions from independent experts.

When it comes to the purchase of an asset which is hoped to provide for their long-term financial future, often far less care is taken. One trip to the local real estate agent, a browse on the internet or even a well-intentioned tip from a mate is all the effort many people make before diving in and committing to one of the largest purchases they will ever make. Worse still are the people who make spontaneous buying decisions while on holidays, at a time when they are feeling relaxed and business calculations are furthest from their minds.

> **Tip!** If you know you will not be able to remain totally unemotional you have even more reason NOT to visit the property. Don't even ask for photographs.

Searching for an investment property using a range of sources is a great place to start, but be aware that it is only the beginning. Once you have a shortlist of possibly acceptable properties your work has just begun.

You must now begin considering the range of possible costs a particular property may incur for you. Then, there are a total of 20 'must ask' questions about property which should be posed and satisfactorily answered before any decisions about which one is right can be made with any certainty. You cannot leave any of these questions out – use the checklist at the end of this section to be sure all of the questions are asked and answered.

What will it cost?

Depending on the type of property you are considering, you can expect a range of costs to both make the purchase and to maintain the property. These will include the following.

Doing the Research

Purchasing costs

1. Conveyancing costs – including labour costs, sundries, postage and photocopying. Anywhere from around $800 to $1,200.

2. Stamp duty on the purchase. This is different for each state but roughly $1,200 for an $80,000 purchase and disproportionately higher as you increase in price. Use Destiny Finsoft to obtain the exact amount for the state in which you are purchasing.

3. Loan stamp duty for the state in which the loan is *settled*. This is also different for each state but approximately $4 per $1,000 borrowed. Be aware that when a loan is written in one state for a property being purchased in another it is usually settled in the purchasing state. Often, stamp duty will be charged in both states, with a refund applied for after the loan has settled in the state where the loan was not written. So, don't be alarmed when two lots of stamp duty appear to have been paid, but do be sure the refund is made.

    Also, in some states a refinance carries no additional stamp duty over and above what has already been paid the first time the debt was incurred (subject to the new loan being for exactly the same purpose). If you have a refinance and a purchase you may be charged full loan stamp duty for the refinance as well as double purchase stamp duty for the two states. A refund will be due for the purchase stamp duty paid in the state where it is not required, and for the amount of the loan stamp duty which was already paid on the part of your refinance loan.

4. Mortgage registration fees for each state in which a mortgage must be registered, around $60 to $80.

5. Title search fees to ensure a clear title. Costs up to $300.

6. Proportionate council and water rates for the remainder of the rated period, refunded to the vendor if already paid.

7. Building and pest inspections, about $250 each.

8. Mine subsidence certificate, if required, about $50.

9. Discharge fees on any loans being paid out, about $150 per loan.

10. Land titles office registration fees, usually under $100.

11. Bank establishment fees and valuation costs of up to $1,000, more if there are additional properties.

12. Body corporate search fees if required. About $300.

13. Quantity surveyors' fees to have a depreciation schedule prepared. About $450.

At the end of this section you will find a buying worksheet to assist you to identify and prepare for these costs. There is a computerised copy of this worksheet contained in your free Destiny Finsoft program too.

Ongoing costs

After you settle, you may have the following ongoing costs:

1. Interest on the loan. Even if you have a principal and interest loan, only the interest portion of the debt is considered an expense as the principal portion is actually buying you ownership.

2. Body corporate fees.

3. Rates, council and water costs.

4. Lawns and garden maintenance.

5. Property management fees for up to 11% of the collected rent.

6. Account keeping fees on the loan.

7. Land tax if applicable.

8. Insurance – building, contents, public liability and landlord's protection.

9. Lease costs and advertising costs.
10. Accountancy costs.
11. Pest control.
12. Security control fees.
13. Cleaning fees.
14. Linen and laundry (for tourism or other niche property).
15. Travel expenses if you make an inspection.
16. Repair costs, depending on the property's age.

Use Worksheet 3.2 at the end of this section to determine all of your possible maintenance costs on each property you may be considering.

Asking the right questions

It can be easy to get caught up in the moment and forget to ask some crucial questions. The following are the 20 questions which you *must* ask. Do not leave any out unless they clearly do not relate to the type of property you are looking at.

1. What is the cash flow of this property?

- Is it positive cash flow?
- Will it remain so in subsequent years – have I done the calculations past year one, taking into account a discount to the allowable claims for each subsequent year?

- If the cash flow is negative, can I afford to support this and additional properties?
- Have I worked out how much margin I have to manage higher interest rates or lower occupancy rates?
- Have I considered all possible costs?

2. *What is the vacancy rate of the area?*

- Visit the Real Estate Institute (REI) website for the state in which you are looking, or call the Institute's offices.
- Telephone local property managers to see how many similar properties are on their books.
- Find out whether quoted occupancy rates on any tourism property can be supported with evidence – check out similar competitors' properties.
- Determine how low you would need to go in rent return in times of low demand and then go back to question one to see if the cash flow is still positive at this low point.

3. *What improvements are being planned for the area?*

- Councils try to provide infrastructure to match a forecast future demand so knowing the council's development plans can help to establish if it expects people to be moving into the area.

- Determine what the developments are. For example, an abundance of retirement villages could mean that the area is aging and this may impact upon tenant supply. Your discovery will also dictate what type of property you should be buying.
- A rock stadium or a garbage tip down the road may impact on future values.

4. What is the population growth?

- Nil or negative population growth means people are moving away and tenant demand is about to suffer.
- If employment opportunities are declining this is also a reliable indicator. Check out the 'Positions Vacant' in the local newspaper.
- High vacancy rates for commercial premises are a sign that commerce is weakening and this may be an indication that the area is about to experience difficulties. If you are buying away from your own area, again look in the local newspaper at commercial vacancies.

5. What is the competition?

- Good population growth and high property demand is not enough – what future development applications have been approved by the council? It could be that you are buying a three bedroom townhouse and there are development applications for another 50 of the same kind of property in the immediate area. Do not forget the recent experience of investors in Sydney and Melbourne city apartments, where a sudden oversupply impacted greatly on what was previously a viable market.

- In the case of tourism property – is the tourism market already catered for? Is occupancy always 100%? If so then this illustrates increasing demand but if the current tourism properties seem to show an increasing struggle to gain occupants this is a sign that there is an oversupply.

6. Is the property tenant friendly?

- Remember, you are not going to live there. Do not be attracted by fancy fixtures and fittings that will be costly to repair and replace – look for standard generic fittings.

- Avoid air conditioning, reticulation, swimming pools, etc. unless absolutely required.

- Landlord's insurance is a must at around $4 a week. This will protect you against loss of rent if the property becomes unable to be tenanted due to damage, as well as pay for the damage to be repaired and any back rent owing.

7. What condition is the property in?

- This can be difficult to ascertain when buying interstate. Start by asking the salesperson.

- Try phoning local property managers, suggesting that you would like them to manage the property if you were to proceed with buying it. Ask if they will go and look at it for you and perhaps even complete a condition report.

- As these two options may not be reliable, always pay to have a building inspection done once you have narrowed the field down to a few choices – this is a cost of investing and is tax deductible.

8. Does it have furniture?

- Furniture can add to your cash flows and allow you to obtain additional rent. It is also depreciable so it allows you more deductions.

- Furniture is not advisable for standard residential properties as most people want to bring their own but it is a must for tourism property and can be useful where the area has an itinerant population. Mining towns are a good example.

9. Is there a body corporate?

- Body corporate fees will lessen your cash flow without adding value in the form of increased rental returns.

- There must be a healthy sinking fund balance, as this is what pays for major repairs. A low sinking fund balance means all owners will have to pay a special levy if a major repair is required, and your contribution will be required regardless of how long you have owned the property.
- Beware of property with low body corporate fees as it could be that not enough is being paid to effectively maintain the common areas.
- Carry out a body corporate search to confirm the financial stability of the body corporate.

10. Is there a rental guarantee?

- Rental guarantees can be offered by people or entities. However, both people and entities regularly go broke, and so these are not really a 'guarantee' at all.
- A guarantee is only a promise which has no regulatory backing. In tough times promises may not be honoured and if the demand for your property is not there you may be left with a white elephant.
- Check the financial backing of guarantors so that you can be sure the money is there to sustain their promises.
- Be sure any guarantee is not just added to your purchase price – this is often the case

and can mean you are buying a property at higher than market value, which subsequently has low demand. This would be a very hard property to sell.

- Where a rental guarantee is a large sum of money placed in trust and used to top up rents, be aware that even a large pot can be used up very quickly if there are a lot of units and high vacancy rates.

11. What is the current property management arrangement?

- What are the experiences and successes of the current property managers and what are all the costs associated with their management? Often a flat rate is quoted as a management fee but additional costs are added – I have seen property management fees blow out to up to 40% of income.

- Where there is some form of on-site manager, ensure you know exactly what the arrangement is and how easy it is to terminate this arrangement if necessary.

- Where there are caretakers, do they have experience and who handles the money?

- Where the management is by way of management rights – what is the experience of the person who has purchased the rights?

What are the costs and what are the termination arrangements?

- For on-site hotel operators, where a large well-known hotel operator is on-site, what is its commercial background and does it have the required experience?

12. Is there a leaseback?

- A leaseback means that an operator becomes your tenant rather than simply operating a letting service for you. You need to know as much about this organisation as you would about any tenant.
- How will the operator fund this leaseback in the event that occupancy is not achieved? Will it have alternative sources of income to support this leaseback?
- What is its financial background?
- Does it have other operations and how financial are they?

13. In the case of a new or off-the-plan property, who are the developers?

- Many a development has not been finished due to liquidation of the developer prior to its completion. What is the financial background of your developer?
- How is it funding the project?

- Who is it using to build – is it a well-known, quality builder?
- Has it built in a margin for cost blowouts?
- How many other developments has it done and has it brought them in on budget?

14. Is there a dual purpose if this is a niche market (purpose built) property?

- Niche market property can often fail if the market has not been sufficiently researched by the developer, or if there is an oversupply.
- Is there a second use for this property? This way, if the original purpose does fail, you can always let out the property as a standard residential rental. The property must lend itself to this purpose.
- Will council allow this change of purpose – often a change in zoning is required before standard residential letting can apply.

15. What is the land availability in the area?

- An abundance of vacant land combined with government and builder incentives may mean that more people own their own home rather than rent and this can affect tenant supply.
- Knowing the demographics of your tenant base can help. Are they likely to be people who wish to own their own home in the area

or are they traditionally renters? The Australian Bureau of Statistics and local councils can provide you with this information.

▸ Scarce land places an upward pressure on prices as well as deepening the tenant pool – look for densely populated areas with no new land available.

16. What is the proximity of the area to a large city?

▸ Large regional areas close to capital cities can satisfy many of the criteria for successful positive cash flow investing as people are forced to look outside of the cities for affordable accommodation. Ensure that the services for easy commuting to the city are in place.

▸ Where prices are still relatively low, the upward pressure on prices in the capital city may be about to flow on – this has always been the case in the past.

▸ Low vacancy rates in cities make tenants look outside cities for property.

17. What is the age of the property?

▸ If a property was built between 1985 and 1987, this means that its building depreciation allowance will be close to finished.

- Older properties without depreciation allowances will need to provide cash flow from rent alone – in other words they will need to be positively geared.

- Older properties will need to have considerations made for higher repair costs so the rent return may need to be a little higher than average – this is often the case anyway in large regional centres as rent return usually relates more to CPI and wages than it does to property prices.

- The local council can tell you accurately when the property was constructed.

18. Is the property at market value?

- What are the recent sales in the area? Listed prices without sales are not an indication of true values – you must know what price comparative properties have actually achieved.

- For tourism property, prices are often set by return. Is the price reasonable for the area? If you pay well over market price for a property just because you believe it will get a higher return, and it subsequently suffers from low occupancy, you may have trouble selling it off as a standard residential property.

19. Is the town you are considering based on just one industry?

▸ Some towns are often built up around a single large company – for example, mining towns.

▸ If everyone in the town works at one company, you can be sure that at some time in the future the company will close and everyone will move out. Be sure there is an alternative source of employment available otherwise you may be left with a property which you cannot rent out or sell.

20. Are you being commercial in your approach?

▸ What is it that attracts you to this property?

▸ Are you attracted by physical features?

▸ Could you easily walk away from this property and not be bothered?

▸ Are you wearing your business hat for this transaction?

> **Tip!** Remember that investment properties are just like city taxis – there is always another one just around the corner!

Once these 20 questions are asked and answered, there is very little that looking at the property can do to change its viability as an investment. You can be safe in the knowledge that you have done as much as you possibly can to maximise the chances of this property being successful for you.

Worksheet 3.1
Property Buying Costs
(Use One for Each Property)

Property costs

Purchase price	
Purchase stamp duty	
Conveyancing costs	
Search fees	
Property building inspection	
Pest inspection	
Mine subsidence certificate	
Land tax certificate	
Council certificates	
Repairs required	
Council and water rates	
Land title registration fees	
Body corporate search fees	
Total	$

cont'd...

Worksheet 3.1 (cont'd): Property Buying Costs

Finance costs

Loan stamp duty	
Loan establishment fee	
Loan settlement fee	
Current debt discharge fees	
Mortgage registration fees	
Total	$

Miscellaneous costs

Cleaning of new property	
Retaining property manager	
Advertising for new tenants	
Lease costs	
Quantity surveyor's report	
Total	$

Total property acquisition costs	$

Worksheet 3.2: Ongoing Costs

Item	$ per annum
Loan interest	
Body corporate fees	
Council rates	
Water rates	
Lawn maintenance	
Property management fees	
Advertising for new tenants	
Leasing costs	
Loan account keeping fees	
Land tax	
Building insurance	
Contents insurance	
Public liability insurance	
Landlord's insurance	
Accountancy costs	
Pest control	
Security control fees	
Cleaning fees	
Linen and laundry	
Travel expenses	
Repair costs	
Total	$

☑ Step 3 Checklist

- ☐ All buying costs calculated – worksheet completed and checked

- ☐ All maintenance costs calculated – worksheet completed, checked and held in file for use after settlement

- ☐ Cash flows calculated as accurately as possible

- ☐ Council phoned and questioned

- ☐ Australian Bureau of Statistics contacted

- ☐ Relevant Real Estate Institute websites checked

- ☐ General information about area sought from internet and other sources

- ☐ Management structure investigated

- ☐ Builder/developer investigated

- ☐ Population and demographics checked for appropriateness

- ☐ Development applications checked to ensure no oversupply

- ☐ Local industry/work availability checked

- ☐ Price of comparative property established

- ☐ Exact age of the property established

☑ *Step 3 Checklist (cont'd)*

- ☐ Condition of property established

- ☐ Lowest rent possible established and property managers checked to ascertain if this rent is possible

- ☐ Local land availability established

- ☐ If it is in a niche market you've checked the property is suitable for alternative use

- ☐ Vacancy rates checked

- ☐ Competition established

- ☐ You've checked that any rental guarantee is sustainable

Step 4

Making Your Choice and Signing Contracts

For many investors, asking the 20 questions posed in Step 3 will narrow down the choices, often to just one or two. For others, there may still be several decisions to make, or the bank may allow for a number of purchases at the one time. Either way, having completed Steps 1 to 3 you are now at the point where you are ready to make an offer and sign contracts on at least one property.

Buying several the same

Often I have seen investors so carried away with what they have discovered about a property that they enthusiastically sign up for two or three of the same type of property, often in the same complex. The promise of a 10% return can sometimes be too irresistible, and if the bank is willing to lend money on several properties at once, some investors feel that it saves time and effort to buy what looks like a viable property investment in bulk.

> **Tip!** When you spread your investments over different areas and property types, the ones which perform really well can support those which don't. You will also find that seasonal highs and lows do not affect you as much.

I caution against ever buying more than one property in the one place for a number of reasons. If the going is great then the decision will have been fortuitous. However, the flip side of that coin is that the effect of a decision to buy a property which fails to deliver on its promise is then compounded several times.

The more important reason is one which relates to growth, and spread. Property definitely behaves in cycles – but not in the same cycles all over the country. To buy all of your property in the one area is the same as putting all of your eggs in the one basket. Property values may rise by 7% in one area and by 15% in another, and if you have all of your property in the 7% area then you have not exposed yourself to the possibility of compounding your gains. As for spread, different property types bring different levels of risk and return. If you can spread your investing over different property types as well as different areas, then the concept of diversification will apply to your property portfolio and you should get a higher than average gain for a lower than average risk.

Choosing the property

Where the answers to your questions have resulted in a clear winner, then the choice will be easy. You may proceed knowing that you have minimised the luck factor and chosen to maximise your chances of success. Where your list still has a number of opportunities which look good, and the bank will not allow you to buy all of them (or you simply don't want to take that big a plunge) then you have a decision to make.

> **Tip!** Cast the net between 50 km and 100 km around capital cities or large regional centres. People will, and do, commute as far as this to work, and once capital cities become too expensive these areas tend to boom in price and population.

Consider the history of the areas in which you are looking, and see which areas have had the most recent 'boom'. In any ten-year period all areas have at least one boom time, and many areas have two. If the properties you are looking at have all satisfied the necessary criteria outlined in the 20 questions from Step 3, and one of the properties is in an area yet to have its boom (or it has been ten years since the last boom), it may be more likely to provide growth.

Note that the criteria for sound investing must still be satisfied – some areas simply never boom, but these areas would also not return the right answers when you ask your 20 questions. Remember those 20 questions have allowed you to narrow down the choice to the properties most likely to grow in value, so choosing the ones yet to boom may be a sound decision and a viable way to prioritise your list.

> **Tip!** Look at an area which has recently experienced an unprecedented boom. Then look at what this area was like before the boom. What did it have which made it suddenly so attractive? Then look to find another area which has these features.

Hopefully you will have ventured outside of your own immediate area, and you may well have found property in another state altogether. As all states have different conveyancing procedures, the steps you take next will vary according to the state.

Making Your Choice and Signing Contracts

Establishing a fair price

When I ask my clients how much their house is worth, they always preface their answer by saying "Well, I would not take any less than...". Usually their estimate is based on what Fred down the road has his house listed for, and on an aesthetic comparison of the two – the client's house may have nicer decorating or be more well kept than Fred's and so this leads to the mistaken notion that one is worth more than the other.

The only true way to gain a handle on the real value of any property is to discover what the recent sales of comparative sized properties have drawn. This is how a valuer will assess any property, and aesthetic features rarely affect the true value.

If you are lucky enough to know a real estate agent, he or she may well be able to print out a listing for you of recent sales in the area. If not, then you may be able to convince a real estate company you are currently dealing with to do so for you. Barring all of that, go back to the internet. Look up a real estate agent with listings in the area in which you are looking, and have a look at its website – often listings show a 'Sold' sign on them, and you can then phone and ask what the sale price was. Once contracts are exchanged or have otherwise become unconditional, this information can be made publicly available. You will then have a fair basis for deciding upon the price you are prepared to pay for the property you are considering, and it is this price on which you can do your calculations to be sure that the property is likely to be cash flow positive.

> **Tip!** When you are between buying properties, keep in touch with what the market is doing by browsing the internet and registering for any online newsletters you can. The Real Estate Institute websites often provide a lot of free information and some which will require a small registration fee.

Negotiating the price

If you have followed all of the steps so far, you will have a priority list of the properties you wish to buy. Unless the property has come to you directly from a developer, in which case there will be little room to move on price, it is now your job to try to obtain that property at a price less than it is being advertised for.

Vendors never place their properties on the market for the actual price they are prepared to take, and buyers never pay what vendors are asking. The price you ultimately pay will depend not only on your skill as a negotiator, but also on the willingness of the vendor to sell quickly.

Making Your Choice and Signing Contracts

A few tips:

- Real estate agents are acting for the vendors, not the purchasers. It does not matter how nice or helpful they are, their commissions are determined by the sale price. Do not ask real estate agents questions like "How keen are they to sell?" or "What is the lowest price they will take?", etc. and expect to get an open and honest answer.

- You should by now have a list of property which suits your requirements. If you have followed the steps closely so far, you should not have become emotional about any of them. Each one should be as good as the next. If you lose one it is not the end of the world, and you can simply move on and negotiate on the next option.

- Be sure the agent knows that you have a number of choices you are currently considering and that the property they have listed is only one of them. This will put you in a position of power.

- Never, ever, show agents that you have become emotional about a property, even if you have. This will provide them with leverage and they will most definitely then begin to play upon your emotions.

- Do all of your negotiations via the telephone and, if possible, screen calls so that when the agent comes back to you with a counter offer you can take some time to call back with an acceptance or rejection. This process is all about keeping the ball in your court.

I normally start by making an offer considerably below the asking price. I base this offer on what I have discovered about recent sales in the area, and usually start at up to $25,000 less than the asking price (depending on the actual price, of course). It is now illegal in most states for a real estate agent not to put all offers up to the vendor, so even a ridiculous offer must be tendered. I do not suggest you waste anyone's time with an outrageous offer but do understand that you have room to move.

Move very slowly toward your final price. Begin by adding just $2,000 to your offer and then go up by only $1,000. Never counter offer as soon as the agent has just delivered the vendor's latest offer to you – this will look like you have not yet reached your final price and it will be reported to the vendor. Always wait at least a day or two before going back with a counter offer.

The risk is, of course, that someone else will come in and pay a higher price and that you will lose the property. Become philosophical about this – if it happens then you were not meant to have the property, and because you have quite a list then it matters little.

> **Tip!** Try to ensure all negotiations are done via phone, fax or the internet. This eliminates the agent's ability to use a personal touch and helps to avoid you becoming prey to a clever salesperson.

I had a client once who used all of the steps to this point very well and unemotionally (although at the point of making the offer she did ask for some photos to be emailed). She used this process of negotiation but the real estate agent was 'double dealing' (playing off two purchasers against each other – most unethical), and she lost the property to someone else.

She called me in tears and I reassured her that there were three other properties on her list that were almost identical to the one she had missed. "But I like *that* one", she said. After a while I was able to get her to see how silly this all was and she ended up buying one of the other properties, for a price below what she was prepared to pay.

> **Tip!** Find four or five properties that you are interested in and make low offers on all of them – that way you will not be focusing on just one property and you may just get a vendor who takes your offer.

Lastly, try to make sure you have the last bid, even if it is $500, or even $200, below the vendor's last counter offer. This keeps you sharp and makes you feel like you have won the battle, even if it was not as resounding a victory as you would have liked.

Signing the contract

The process by which contracts are put into effect differs from state to state. As you may well be buying outside of your own area, it will be useful to fully understand the procedures required in each state.

New South Wales

A New South Wales contract is known as a 'Contract of Sale'. By law this must be prepared before a property is even placed on the market, and it contains all of the relevant disclosure statements. It is then freely available to be looked over as soon as a price is agreed upon, or even before so if you wish.

New South Wales contracts are not legally binding until they are 'exchanged' (a process whereby the solicitors of each party meet and swap contracts, along with a deposit of up to 10% of the purchase price) and at any stage up to exchange the deal is not finalised – anyone can come along and buy the property out from under you (a move known as 'gazumping'). While it is an unspoken ethic that a real estate agent will not show the property to any

Making Your Choice and Signing Contracts

new buyers while it is under negotiation, the practice can often be the reverse, as unscrupulous agents attempt to push buyers into decisions by introducing competition to the transaction.

> **Tip!** Never exchange or go unconditional on any contract prior to having a full loan approval from your lender.

Prior to exchange, you are wise to have a pest and building inspection carried out to uncover any major faults. Once exchanged, you do have a five-day cooling off period in which you can pull out for any reason, however, if the inspections take longer than this you have no opportunity to rescind. You can also waive your cooling off period or sign a contract 'on a 0.25%', which is real estate speak indicating that you secure the property, pay 0.25% of the purchase price as an initial deposit and then work toward full exchange. This prevents the vendor from selling to anyone else but you lose your 0.25% in the event that you rescind.

> **Tip!** Visit a lender prior to beginning your search and get some kind of conditional approval in place. This may save you time once contracts are signed and relieve some of the pressure that can be placed on you at this early stage.

Victoria

Victorian purchasers also have a 'Contract for Sale' prepared. However, before making any offers they are provided with a 'Vendor's Statement', which covers all of the relevant information they must know about a property including building permits issued, covenants, services details, etc.

Purchasers read these statements before making offers, which are then written into a 'Contract Note' and forwarded with a deposit to vendors or their solicitors. The Contract Note is a legal document which is binding once signed by a vendor.

In some cases this Contract Note forms the only contract, in others an actual Contract for Sale is prepared. Be aware that signing a Contract Note means that you, as the purchaser, are agreeing to any general conditions which will be in the Contract for Sale, such as penalty rates if settlement is delayed, statements that the vendor is to provide good title, provision to pay by cash or bank cheque and a statement that the buyer has 21 days to arrange 'requisitions on title' (specific details about the property and its title).

If you want to include conditions in a sale (such as a subject to finance clause, or a request for any repairs to be made prior to settlement) then these must be included in the Contract Note.

Australian Capital Territory

ACT conveyancing procedures involve the preparation of Contracts for Sale and exchange of these contracts is required. However offers are all verbal and there is no cooling off period. Purchasers are vulnerable to being 'gazumped' as Contracts for Sale are not available until about ten days after the offer has been made.

Northern Territory

While the offer process in the Northern Territory is verbal, an 'Offer to Purchase' must be signed once a price has been agreed. This is not a legal document however, and no protection to the purchaser exists until a contract is drawn up, signed and exchanged.

South Australia

Once a reasonable offer has been made a contract is drawn up which includes all conditions and outlines the deposit payable and the settlement date. Once signed by both parties it becomes binding and no 'exchange' is required. Cooling off does apply in South Australia.

Western Australia

Once you have decided to negotiate on a property in Western Australia this is done via an 'Offer and Acceptance' form. This is a two-page document completed by the real estate agent, with your offer written in the space provided. The agent takes this to the vendor, who either signs to accept your offer, or crosses out your offer and writes in a counter offer. This can go back and forward with much crossing out until both parties agree on the price and then sign the form. Note that this form must include all conditions, and the signing by the vendor is an agreement to not only the price but to any listed conditions as well. It is a binding agreement which becomes unconditional once all of the conditions have been satisfied, and there is no cooling off period.

Queensland

Probably due to the huge issues which have been raised by two tier marketing and other questionable real estate practices in Queensland, there now exists a rather cumbersome process for purchasing in this state.

It proceeds as follows:

1. Request a Property Agents and Motor Dealers Act (PAMD) form 27A on any property you like. This form discloses any material interests or relationships the selling agent has in the sale.

2. Obtain a PAMD form 30A, which is a warning statement from the selling agent drawing your

attention to important contractual obligations, such as cooling off periods, etc.

3. Make your offer.
4. Sign a 'Contract for Sale' (note that in Queensland the period in which you may obtain finance approval is a standard two weeks, after which the contract is void) and pay a deposit.
5. If the offer is accepted, the vendor and purchaser must both sign PAMD form 31A, which is a declaration from the seller letting the buyer know the date the contract was signed.
6. Five-day cooling off period begins unless purchasers have signed a PAMD form 32A which waives their rights to cooling off.

The resulting contract is then binding and you can proceed to settlement.

Tasmania

What a great place to buy property! You make your offer on a 'Contract for Sale' which, once signed by the vendor, becomes the binding contract. There is no cooling off period.

Table 4.1, at the end of this section has been reproduced from *How to Create an Income for Life* and is a ready reckoner which shows you what is required, state by state. Refer to this when you choose your property so you will know exactly what steps you need to take next.

In whose name?

The question of whose name and under what tenancy arrangement you should buy the property, will be dealt with in Step 8, which looks at taxation. A comprehensive analysis is also provided from page 183 of *How to Create an Income for Life*. Nevertheless, you will need to have some basic idea at this stage as to whose name you want to buy in, because the contracts must be signed in the correct names to avoid costly changes later. So let's have a brief look at the issue.

In a nutshell the following applies:

▸ Do you wish your share of the property to fall to the other owner(s) automatically upon your death and will all owners hold equal shares? If "Yes", then you should buy as joint tenants, as this means that shares in a property fall outside your estate upon death and go automatically to the other party(ies).

▸ Do you want to will your share to someone else and/or do you want unequal shares in the new property? If "Yes", then you should buy as tenants in common as this not only means that your share falls within your estate, and so can be included in your will, but it also means you can specify a percentage ownership for each party. You might choose this where you want one party to receive more of the income, and more of the tax benefits than the other party.

- Is the property positively geared (raw rent return is more than raw expenses and there are not enough tax deductions to wipe out your gain, so you will make a taxable income)? If "Yes", then buy the property in the lowest income earner's name.

- Is the property negatively geared, or does it have a positive cash flow only because of the tax deductions? If "Yes", then buy the property in the higher income earner's name.

- If all incomes are in the same tax bracket, then joint ownership can apply under either joint tenants or tenants in common.

Note that any property purchased as a sole tenant will become part of that person's estate upon his or her death.

Paying the deposit

The deposit required may be anything from $1,000 right up to 10% of the purchase price, payable upon exchange or when contracts become unconditional.

This is all very well if you happen to have $10,000 to $20,000 lying about in a bank account, but the realities are that most people today are using the equity in existing property to form the deposit on new property purchases. While some people may have a line of credit in place with sufficient funds available to pay any required deposits, this is not always the case. If you have trouble raising a deposit, it may be possible to ask the vendor to accept a less than standard amount, but where there is an abundance of available buyers for a property this is unlikely to be agreed upon.

> **Tip!** Prior to commencing your search for property, remember to start a Property Portfolio File which includes all of the paperwork you might need – including loan applications and deposit bond forms. If you partially complete them before you are ready to transact it will save time when you do need them.

For a fee, which is usually only about 5% of the deposit required, you can obtain what is known as a 'deposit bond'. Put simply, a deposit bond is an assurance by an insurance company that if, for some reason, you renege on the deal prior to settlement and so forfeit the deposit (which of course you have not paid), the insurance company will pay the

Making Your Choice and Signing Contracts

amount of the deposit to the vendor, who of course is able to keep this (under the rules of the contract).

A deposit bond does not relieve you of the financial responsibility, however, as the insurance company will then sue you to recover the full amount of the deposit. Deposit bonds are usually only available to applicants who complete an application and satisfy a range of criteria including a credit reference check. They can, however, provide an excellent tool for purchasing property without a cash deposit.

Worksheet 4.1
Special Conditions List

Use the following space to note the special conditions which are attached to your contract and include the latest date for satisfaction of these conditions. Be sure to check this list periodically to ensure these conditions are met:

1. ....

   ....

   to be met by (date) ..../......./..........

2. ....

   ....

   to be met by (date) ..../......./..........

3. ....

   ....

   to be met by (date) ..../......./..........

4. ....

   ....

   to be met by (date) ..../......./..........

Table 4.1
State-by-State Purchase Contract Requirements

Item	NSW	WA	ACT	Vic.	NT	SA	Qld	Tas.
Offer and acceptance	No	Yes	No	Contract Note	Yes	No	Yes	No
Separate vendor's statement	No	No	No	Yes	No	No	Yes	No
Offer contract final	No	Yes	No	No	No	Yes	Yes	Yes
Special conditions	No	Yes	Yes	Yes	Yes	Yes	Yes	Yes
Exchange required	Yes	No	Yes	Yes	Yes	No	No	No
Cooling off	Yes	No	No	Yes	Yes	Yes	Yes	No
Conveyancers allowed	Yes	Yes	Yes	For non-legal work	Yes	Yes	No	No
Gazumping	Yes	No	Yes	Yes	Yes	No	Yes	No

☑ *Step 4 Checklist*

- ☐ Properties chosen from a number of different areas
- ☐ Properties prioritised according to ability to answer the 20 questions in Step 3
- ☐ Decision made about whose name in which to purchase
- ☐ Decision made about joint tenancy or tenants in common
- ☐ Contract for Sale form requested (NSW, ACT, SA, Tas.)
- ☐ Contract for Sale explained/read thoroughly (NSW, ACT, SA, Tas.)
- ☐ All required conditions of sale including a 'subject to finance' clause noted on contracts (NSW, ACT, SA, Tas.)
- ☐ Contract for Sale signed (SA, Tas.)
- ☐ Conditions for contract met (SA, Tas.)
- ☐ Contract for Sale signed and exchanged (NSW, ACT)
- ☐ Contract Note requested (Vic.)
- ☐ Contract Note read/explained thoroughly (Vic.)

Making Your Choice and Signing Contracts

☑ *Step 4 Checklist (cont'd)*

☐ Contract Note signed (Vic.)

☐ Contract for Sale read/signed (Vic.)

☐ Special conditions noted (WA)

☐ Special conditions satisfied within timeframes (WA)

☐ Offer to purchase signed (NT)

☐ Contract for Sale read and signed (NT)

☐ PAMD forms 27A and 30A requested, read and signed (Qld)

☐ Offer accepted, PAMD form 31A requested and signed (Qld)

☐ Contracts read/signed (Qld)

☐ If applicable, cooling off waived via PAMD form 32A

☐ Deposit bond applied for

☐ Deposit bond received

☐ Contracts finalised (all states)

Step 5

Applying for Finance

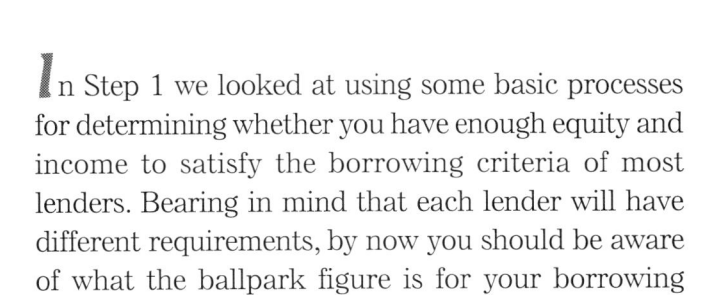

In Step 1 we looked at using some basic processes for determining whether you have enough equity and income to satisfy the borrowing criteria of most lenders. Bearing in mind that each lender will have different requirements, by now you should be aware of what the ballpark figure is for your borrowing power at this time.

Once you have decided on the property you want to buy, you should not begin the conveyancing process until you have the loan application in progress. This is because many things can happen to delay the process of obtaining a loan, and if your finance is delayed you may then miss crucial dates which could cause your contract to fall over. While in most cases a new contract can be prepared and signed, this may add cost and stress to the process and leave you vulnerable in the event that other buyers are on the waiting list for the same property.

This section will cover everything you must do to apply for a loan. However, before looking at the actual process, let's look at what type of loan you need for your investment portfolio.

Which loan?

With literally thousands of products available from around 50 possible lenders, you could be forgiven for feeling confused about which loan is best for you. If you use brokers, chances are they may be recommending the best loans for them, based on the commissions they will receive. If you are approaching lenders directly, their managers will only be able to recommend what they feel is the best of their available products – but their loans may not stack up at all against those of their competitors.

> **Tip!** It is the purpose of the loan, not what secures it, which determines whether it is tax deductible.

In any case, it is rare to find staff members who are actually fully informed about the taxation implications of the type and structure of their loans. While their product knowledge may be superb, few mortgage brokers or bank managers can truly advise you of the right loan and structure for you, regardless of how professional and helpful they may seem.

One of the main issues here is that, once set, it can be difficult to reset a loan which is wrong for you, especially where the problem lies in the actual structure (that is, in whose name the purchase was made, etc.). So, rather than trust those trying to assist you, it is far better to understand these things for yourself. A full explanation of loan types, loan structures and their appropriateness for you can be found in *How to Create an Income for Life* (Chapter 9). The following is some brief information to assist you with your choice.

> **Tip!** Using a loan broker who is also a financial or property adviser will ensure that you get the right loan and structure for your personal circumstances. Bank managers and standard loan brokers usually do not have the knowledge or expertise you need.

Interest-only or principal and interest (P&I)

An interest-only loan is any loan which only requires a repayment equal to the interest accrued for that month. These loans usually come with a term, although some 'lines of credit' (which are essentially interest-only loans) are perpetual. A P&I loan, on the other hand, is a loan which requires a payment covering all of the interest and enough of the principal to finalise the loan in the pre-agreed period – usually 25 to 30 years.

Most investors are confused about which one to choose. Property salespeople often suggest interest-only as they know that this makes the commitment appear smaller and can make their sales job easier. Bank managers usually suggest P&I so that at least the loan will get paid off at some point and they will recoup their money.

There is a simple way to work out which is right for you by answering the following two questions:

1. *Do you have a debt on your own home?*

If "Yes", then get an interest-only loan on your investment debts, and be sure to make principal and interest repayments to your personal debts (including extra repayments as often as possible) until you have no personal debt. Then do the same with your investment debts.

If "No", then get a principal and interest debt for your new investments and pay as much money as you can afford into it as often as you can.

This can be taken one step further and this next step depends on your answer to another question.

Applying for Finance

2. Are you a good money manager and do you trust yourself with money?

If "No", then be sure to have at least one principal and interest debt, as above, at all times.

If "Yes", then forget the P&I versus interest-only argument and just get yourself a line of credit. This gives you the flexibility to pay all of your money into the debt (and get it out again if you need to). It will offset and minimise interest, vastly reducing the term and cost of all of your loans and allowing you to gain maximum property equity in minimum time.

Be very careful though – you have to work to a budget and be sure that you do not abuse a product such as this. If you are going to use a line of credit product, the correct structure is crucial to ensure you maximise every dollar and stay on the right side of the tax department.

> **Tip!** A line of credit must have the option to split your funds into accounts for different purposes, and your investment funds must be kept separate to personal borrowings. Page 153 of *How to Create an Income for Life* gives an illustration of how this should be done.

All three of my property books explore lines of credit in explicit detail with *How to Maximise Your*

Property Portfolio (page 147) outlining a unique way that we have assisted our clients to satisfy tax office requirements while still applying rapid mortgage reduction principles to investment debt.

Fixed or variable?

At the time of writing there have been some interest rate rises and the fear is that more are to follow. This has resulted in an avalanche of applications from investors to fix the interest rate of their loans.

I am still not personally convinced that we should rush out to fix the interest rate on our loans. This is because the fixed rates are always higher than the variable rates and the expected rises, at this stage, seem as if they will not be too great.

In addition, fixed-rate loans usually carry harsh financial penalties for early discharge, and you cannot make changes to these loans once they are set. If I were to fix my loans now, at a higher rate than I pay on a variable rate, the extra money I pay now may well be more than the extra I would pay if I just sat on a variable rate and absorbed any increases or decreases. I also cannot know what is around the corner and what kind of adjustment I may need to make to my loan portfolio to accommodate future investing.

As an investor, you must also remember that any interest rate rise actually has less impact on you, as interest is a tax-deductible cost. So, depending on your own marginal rate of tax, the effective rate rise for you may only be half of the actual rise.

You must decide personally how you feel. Consider the following questions:

1. Will you feel more comfortable knowing that you have a set rate of interest?

2. Are you prepared for the fact that interest rates may not rise too much and you will end up paying more?

3. In the event that you are not sure, have you considered fixing only part of your loan?

Don't forget that you can fix a rate at any time during your loan term. So, if the predictions are suddenly that we will see a serious increase to interest rates, you can immediately lock in the day's fixed rate simply by visiting your bank or broker.

Be aware, however, that most lenders are now offering two ways to fix an interest rate – one via a 'fixed rate' and one via a 'rate lock'. Fixed rate means that the fixed rate *at the time of loan settlement* will apply and the rate lock means that the fixed rate *at the time of applying for a fixed rate* will apply.

Usually you must pay a fee on the spot for the rate lock, while the fixed rate requires payment upon settlement.

What will banks accept as security?

Generally speaking, banks will accept the following property types as security for borrowings:

- Residential houses and units over 50 square metres
- Rural properties or land
- Vacant land
- Commercial or industrial premises (although these usually require a commercial loan)
- Holiday houses or units satisfying the criteria for residential lending.

Some lenders may lend on the following, although often at a reduced loan to valuation ratio (LVR) – often as little as 50%:

- Residential houses or units under 50 square metres
- Serviced apartments over 50 square metres.

You will be hard pressed to find a lender that will lend on:

- Hotel rooms
- Serviced apartments under 50 square metres
- Transportable homes or trailers
- Retirement or student accommodation which is purpose built.

If you choose to buy a property which no lender will lend against, you will only be able to do so where you have ample equity in existing property to support the loan without the new property being used as security. In these cases, the expected income from the new property may also not be acknowledged by the bank, so you must be able to service the loan with existing income. *How to Maximise Your Property Portfolio* (page 65) covers the risks associated with using other property to secure a purchase which is not acknowledged by a lender.

Acceptable income

Again all lenders will differ in terms of what they will accept as income. The following list usually applies:

- Income from full-time or permanent part-time employment
- 50% of casual income
- Income from social security if in addition to the above income
- Family payments (sometimes limited to children under ten)
- Commission income if proven by at least two years of tax returns
- Self-employed income after two to three years of trading

- 80% of income from rental properties where proven
- 80% of prospective income on a new property purchase
- Pension or annuity income where additional to main source of income.

Some lenders may also accept the following:

- Bonus payments if proven to be regular
- Regular overtime (usually only 50% accepted)
- Shift allowances
- Other irregular income.

The loan procedure

To help you understand and track your finance a little more easily, the following steps, and their relative applicable timeframes (in working days) are usually taken by most lenders. Some lenders will have slightly different procedures but, generally speaking, the process will be:

1. Application submitted with all required documentation (two days).
2. Conditional approval given 'subject to' – this means that any outstanding documentation must be supplied, incomes verified with employers, valuations completed (for

Applying for Finance

purchases a valuation is usually only carried out if the loan is more than 80% of the purchase price, for existing security property a valuation is always carried out). Sometimes other criteria apply to a conditional approval and the particular conditions will be up to the lender. (One to three days.)

3. Valuations ordered and performed. Where a valuation exists which is not more than 12 months old this may be able to be used, otherwise additional valuations will be required. (Two to five days.)

4. Unconditional approval issued (one to two days).

5. Loan contracts (loan offer documents) issued and forwarded to customer (received within four days).

6. Loan contracts signed and returned to lender (two to four days).

7. Mortgage documents prepared (two to five days).

8. Mortgage documents forwarded to customer (received within four days).

9. Mortgage documents returned to lender (two to five days).

10. If straight purchase, lender will be ready to settle within three to five days of receiving completed

mortgage documents as long as all conditions for advancing the loan have been met.

11. If other loans need to be discharged, lender will contact discharging bank to obtain payout figures. This is where it can all go terribly wrong as lenders can play games and do all they can to prevent a loan from being discharged. You may be contacted by your bank for an interview at which a staff member will attempt to retain your business (albeit a little late). This process can take up to two or even three weeks.

From this rough guide you can see that 35 working days (seven weeks) is a reasonable timeframe in which to expect a new loan to settle, with unconditional approval taking anything up to 12 to 14 working days (or three weeks). Where existing loans also need to be discharged, a further three weeks may be added. You can assist in many ways by being prepared for this process and having all of your documentation ready, signing anything you receive in a timely fashion and, where possible, express posting or hand delivering documents to cut out any further delays.

> **Tip!** Finance is an area where everything can easily go wrong – be prepared for extensive delays!

The process to apply

1. Choose lender and loan type

You should research lenders and loan types prior to even choosing an investment property. When you are calculating your borrowing capacity (Step 1) ensure that you find out as much as you can about different lenders and the loans they have to offer. Don't fall into the trap of choosing the lender you are currently with just because it has been good to you. Lenders are paid to be good to you and your current lender may not have the best product for your personal circumstances. It is also important to have done your research as you do not want to waste valuable time applying to a lender with whom you will not qualify anyway.

How to Make Your Money Last as Long as You Do (Chapter 4) outlines all of the questions you should ask each bank about its loan products. These questions are reproduced at the end of this section. Be sure that you do not take any financial advice from brokers or bank managers unless they are clearly qualified to give it to you. Few organisations truly know about successful property investing and any advice you will get from these people may be subjective or simply wrong.

Another important point is to remember that, just because your current lender will not give you any further borrowings, this does not mean you cannot invest further. A multi-lender strategy works beautifully where your current lender will not advance further borrowings, or where it will not accept a particular property you have chosen as security. *How to Create an Income for Life* (pages 196 and 197) covers the best way to structure a multi-lender loan portfolio.

> **Tip!** Banks usually do not like to provide second mortgages over property.

2. Submit application

Completing bank applications can be tiresome, however you can minimise the stress by being prepared prior to actually making the application. The following is a list of documentation you must have available for the bank. Having these documents ready beforehand will ensure that the process is handled more quickly.

1. 100 points of identification if applying to a new bank.
    i. Birth certificate or passport (70 points)
    ii. Driver's licence and other photo identification (40 points)
    iii. Medicare cards, credit cards, library cards, etc. (25 points)

Applying for Finance

    iv. Rates notices or energy notices (10 points).

2. Statements for the last 12 months of payments on any existing mortgages. These are to prove good conduct. They must be consecutive statements – any missing ones may alert the bank to a problem.

3. Statements for the last three months of credit card or personal loan payments.

4. Proof of income. Original pay slips, tax returns if self-employed, evidence of overtime and bonuses or property rental statements.

5. Rates notices on all properties to confirm title details.

6. Where a new rental property is being purchased, proof of its potential rental income (usually a letter from a local real estate agent will suffice).

7. Social security notices if you are receiving benefits and this income is needed to service the debt.

8. Any hire-purchase contracts.

9. Evidence of any gifts where part of a deposit is being gifted.

10. Full details of property being purchased.

11. Copies of front page (details page) of purchase contracts.

> **Tip!** Usually lenders will not accept forecasts of rental income, especially where the income is for a tourism property and it is way above standard residential returns. However, they may accept a letter from a local agent with an opinion of market rent.

Of course there is a range of 'low doc' options available at the time of writing. These are loans that require a minimum of documentation and can be of use to people who have an income that is difficult to substantiate. Be aware that these types of loans usually come with a premium in the form of a higher interest rate or a higher establishment fee, or both.

You will be required to sign a declaration, stating that all of the information supplied by you is true and correct, and also sign an authority so that the bank may carry out a Credit Advantage Limited (CAL) check. CAL (now Baynet) holds a lot of information about you, and if you have ever defaulted on a loan or had other difficulties with borrowed money, this is where the details will be found. Be sure to be open and honest with your bank – an entry to your file at Baynet will not necessarily result in a loan being declined, especially if you have openly disclosed the details and shown to the bank that the matter has been rectified.

Applying for Finance

Ensure that you have made arrangements for all valuations to be carried out. This includes contacting the managing agent of any current rental properties you own to advise that a valuer will be calling and to ensure that his access is made possible. Ask the property manager to give your tenants notice of an impending valuation even before the valuer actually makes contact.

Keep current copies of all of the above documentation in your 'Property Portfolio File' along with loan applications which are semi-completed. This way you will be ready to spring into action as soon as you find the right property. At the end of this section you will find an application checklist. Keep this in your file and use it for every application you make.

> **Tip!** Even if you have a default noted on your credit reference, being upfront with the bank about this before it discovers the problem may be enough to convince your lender to give you another chance.

3. Keep in touch with your lender and sign all documentation

Bearing in mind the timeframes outlined previously, you must keep in touch with your lender or broker to be sure that there are not additional requests which you must meet. You are not the only client it has and no matter how efficient it is, your loan is not necessarily the top of its priority list. Of course, be careful you do not become too annoying – there is no use contacting the lender prior to a timeframe even expiring as the staff there will have nothing to tell you. However, if a timeframe passes with no contact then, by all means, make a call.

When you receive loan documents or any other documents, take action on them immediately and, if possible, hand deliver them to save vital time. Where you are also discharging other loans at the same time that you are making a new purchase, ensure that you visit your current lender and sign any required documentation to enable it to release the mortgage. These are known as 'Authority to Discharge' forms and each lender will insist you sign one before it will release your securities.

> **Tip!** Before a bank will settle a loan it must have a certificate of currency for the required building insurance amount, which cites the bank as the 'interested party'. Be sure to arrange this with your insurer.

As previously mentioned, be very sure you know the dates of events that are crucial to your loan – as listed in the Step 4 checklist. If you have a particular

Applying for Finance

date for notification that finance is approved, you must meet this. Inform your broker or lender of your critical dates – attach the form included at the end of this section when you submit your loan application as this will ensure that the lender's attention is drawn to vital information about your new property, in addition to any other important details.

Worksheet 5.1:
Mortgage Loan Application Checklist

Att NA General

☐ ☐ Completed and signed mortgage loan application.

☐ ☐ Completed 'Funds to Complete' worksheet.

☐ ☐ 100 points of identification provided.

☐ ☐ Completed funds to complete worksheet.

Proof of Income Provided for Each Applicant

☐ ☐ PAYG – Letter of employment (maximum four weeks old and must be on company letterhead) – only acceptable if computerised pay slips are not available, and in such cases two years of income tax returns or group certificates would also need to be provided.

☐ ☐ OR three x original pay slips (must be originals and no greater than four weeks old).

☐ ☐ If overtime is required for serviceability, last year's tax return must be supplied to confirm total yearly income.

☐ ☐ If any applicant is a director of a company and requires not only his/her wage but also the company profits to qualify for the finance, all directors of the company will be required to be guarantors on the loan.

☐ ☐ Accountant's name and telephone number for each self-employed applicant.

cont'd...

Worksheet 5.1 (cont'd): Mortgage Loan Application Checklist

Att NA

☐ ☐ Self-employed or company income – three years of full returns required including balance sheets and profit and loss statements for the company or business, as well as three years of full personal returns are also required. Note: if the business is less than two years old and/or financials are more than three months old, then interims (profit and loss) will be required. If these interims are substantially different from the tax return and this income is required for loan serviceability then the bank may reject the application or ask for a 'please explain' the difference.

☐ ☐ Letter from Centrelink if social security is required for serviceability (note: not all financial institutions accept Centrelink payments).

☐ ☐ Rental income: Letter from managing agent OR rental statements OR letter from agent regarding potential rent if not currently rented.

☐ ☐ Telephone numbers and addresses of employees (other than the current one) for the past three years.

Proof of Good Conduct on All Current Loans

☐ ☐ 12 months of statements on each mortgaged loan OR a letter from the bank manager confirming good conduct on each loan with no arrears.

cont'd...

Worksheet 5.1 (cont'd): Mortgage Loan Application Checklist

Att NA

☐ ☐ Statements for six months of payments on credit cards, personal loans and leases.

☐ ☐ A letter for any other loans with no statements, such as a copy of the contract for car loans or interest free loans.

☐ ☐ Statements for payments of three months if not refinancing, and six months if refinancing, of statements on store accounts.

☐ ☐ Details on any outstanding rates.

☐ ☐ Information about any loans, especially those with caveats, which have been completed in the last three years.

☐ ☐ Information on any loans which have been applied for but not taken up in the last three years.

☐ ☐ If either client is self-employed or a director of a company, disclose details of any finance obtained or applied for as a director.

☐ ☐ If either client has been in default of a loan or had an entry on their CAL for late payment, an explanation in writing will be required.

Mortgage Security

☐ ☐ Rates notices on all properties to be used as security for the loan.

cont'd...

Worksheet 5.1 (cont'd):
Mortgage Loan Application Checklist

Att NA

☐ ☐ Full details of all security properties.

☐ ☐ Full details of access to security properties for valuation – contact name, telephone numbers, address details.

Property Purchase

☐ ☐ Copy of front page of Contract of Sale

☐ ☐ Proof of deposit where client is using own funds.

☐ ☐ Evidence of savings deposit – six months savings statements if savings shown on application form.

☐ ☐ Confirmation of names to appear on the title/s.

Construction Loans

☐ ☐ Written tender, building plans and specifications (tender must reflect builder's licence number).

Account Information

☐ ☐ Number of accounts required.

☐ ☐ Ownership details of each account in application (names to appear on the accounts).

☐ ☐ Limits of each account in application.

cont'd...

Worksheet 5.1 (cont'd): Mortgage Loan Application Checklist

Att NA Credit Card Application

☐ ☐ Signed application form with credit card limit requested.

Miscellaneous Information

☐ ☐ Details about the purpose of additional funds where the amount applied for exceeds the amount required for the purchase and/or refinance.

☐ ☐ If a maximum lend is being applied for, details of which account limits should be altered if the valuation or serviceability calculation is different than expected, are required.

© Destiny Financial Solutions 2004

Applying for Finance

Bank Name: ....

Please note that the following information is crucial to this loan:

1. Latest date that we can have an unconditional approval:……../………/…….

2. Date on which this loan must settle …./……./….

3. Other loans which must be discharged:

i. Lender:............................Loan #:.............
ii. Lender:............................Loan #:.............
iii. Lender:............................Loan #:.............

4. Contacts for valuations:

Property:...
Contact:......................……….. Ph: ....
Special access information: ....

Property:...
Contact:......................……….. Ph:....................
Special access information: ....

5. Special notes for this loan:

....
....
....

Worksheet 5.2:
Questions to Ask Your Bank

Questions to ask about a P&I loan

1. What is the method for calculation of interest?
2. How much does it cost to fix the rate on my loan after the loan has been taken out?
3. What fees are associated with this loan: application, establishment, valuation, settlement, mortgage preparation and all other fees as well as monthly fees?
4. Is there a limit to the amount of extra repayments I can make?
5. How often do I get statements?
6. Is there a charge for swapping to a different type of loan in the future?
7. Is there a charge for discharging the mortgage?
8. Do I have to pay a fee to the bank when I discharge the loan?
9. Is there a penalty for early repayment?

Questions to ask the bank about an interest-only loan:

1. Can I repay any of the principal during the interest-only term? If "Yes", is there a limit to the amount and/or a penalty?
2. Is it easy to renegotiate this loan into another type of loan?
3. Is the interest rate comparable to other loan products?

cont'd...

Worksheet 5.2 (cont'd): Questions to Ask Your Bank

Questions to ask the bank about an interest-only loan (cont'd):

4. What are the fees involved in setting up/switching to another product at the end of the fixed term?
5. Is there a penalty for early repayment?
6. How long is the term before the loan is to be renegotiated?

Questions to ask the bank about line of credit loans:

1. How is the interest rate calculated?
2. Is it a true line of credit – do I have full access to the full original amount at all times or are principal reductions required? (If so, this is NOT a line of credit.)
3. Is the loan transferable from property to property?
4. Is there a term and a penalty for early repayments?
5. Can I split the loan for multipurposes?
6. Can I apply different features to each split?
7. What are the transaction fees?
8. Is there a cheque book attached to the loan? If so, is this optional? (If it is a 'cheque' account, you will pay additional government fees on debits.)

☑ *Step 5 Checklist*

- ☐ Lender chosen
- ☐ Loan product chosen
- ☐ Rate lock chosen and paid for if applicable
- ☐ Fixed rate chosen if applicable
- ☐ Loan application completed
- ☐ Loan application, declaration and CAL check authority signed
- ☐ Statements for 12 months of payments collected on all mortgages
- ☐ Statements collected for three months of payments on all credit cards and other loans
- ☐ Proof of all income
- ☐ Rental statements
- ☐ Social security statements
- ☐ Proof of expected rental income
- ☐ Proof of bonuses
- ☐ Tax returns of self-employed
- ☐ Hire-purchase contracts
- ☐ Evidence of gifts if applicable

Applying for Finance

☑ *Step 5 Checklist (cont'd)*

- ☐ 100 points of ID supplied
- ☐ Details of property to be purchased included in loan application
- ☐ Loan application submitted ……../……./…… (note date)
- ☐ Progress checked after three days
- ☐ Conditional loan approval received
- ☐ Arrangements made for someone to meet valuer on all properties
- ☐ Unconditional loan approval received
- ☐ Authority to discharge form signed at old bank
- ☐ Loan contracts received
- ☐ Loan contracts signed and returned ……../ ………./…….. (note date)
- ☐ Mortgage documents received
- ☐ Mortgage documents signed and returned ……./……../…..(note date)
- ☐ Certificate of currency received from insurer
- ☐ Loan settled
- ☐ Accounts checked for accuracy

Step 6

The Conveyancing Process

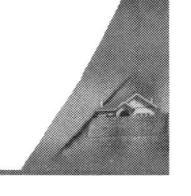

You probably think that, as you now appear to be on the home straight, you can breathe a little more easily and sit back, waiting for your property to settle. Wrong! This is when the hardest work begins.

Until this point things have been fairly straightforward – now you must get the property settled, get it managed and then tackle the arduous task of preparing for your first tax return.

We have already covered the process of signing contracts and pointed out the differences in the contracts used within each state. After a contract has exchanged, or become unconditional, the processes followed to settle a property are very similar all over Australia.

Should I use a lawyer?

This depends very much on where the property is situated. In Western Australia, conveyancing is almost exclusively managed by what are known as 'settlement agents'. While they do not have law degrees, they will have undergone an extensive education program that includes property law. The beauty of a settlement agent is that the resulting cost of conveyancing is far less in Western Australia than in any other state.

In New South Wales, the ACT, Northern Territory and South Australia you may, if you wish, choose to use a conveyancer rather than a solicitor and sometimes this minimises your costs a little. Conveyancers will have had similar educations to settlement agents and they are certainly adequate for the task. If the property you are buying has a complex management structure, however, or some kind of income pooling arrangement or other unusual feature, I recommend using a solicitor as you may need additional legal advice about matters other than simple property issues.

> **Tip!** If you are buying a standard residential property a conveyancer will be sufficient. If the property you are considering is anything else, you may wish to choose a reputable legal firm to be sure that you receive good quality advice.

In Victoria, you can use a conveyancer, but only for any non-legal work. Conveyancers in Victoria normally have some kind of arrangement with a local solicitor who will carry out the legal work, usually for a set fee.

Queensland and Tasmania are yet to allow the use of any professionals other than solicitors for property conveyancing. The process for buying in Queensland has undergone a rigorous overhaul as a result of the problems experienced in recent years at the hands of Queensland property developers.

The conveyancing process

Once you have signed the contracts and they have become unconditional, the following procedure will begin.

1. Searches carried out

Some searches are undertaken prior to the contracts becoming unconditional. Others will be carried out afterwards. The main searches that are carried out are a title search and a government authority search, which ensures there are no nasty surprises about future plans for your property

As this is an automatic part of conveyancing, you should not need to make any requests for these searches, with the exception of a body corporate search. This is not a standard search and you will have to pay an additional (very worthwhile) fee for this to be carried out.

Other possible searches include:

- Company search
- Contaminated land search
- Land tax search
- Registered plan search.

You conveyancer can advise if these will be required in your case. Less common searches include:

- Bankruptcy search
- Heritage search
- Limited town planning certificate search
- Mines search
- Rails search
- Water metre readings.

Again, you must be guided by your legal representative as to which of these you will need, and what the costs of each will be.

> **Tip!** Although you are paying for someone else to carry out your conveyancing, it is useful to track the process yourself. There are countless times that I have called conveyancers only to find that they have not yet completed a step, with the latest date for doing so looming.

2. Requisitions on title

At this stage your solicitor or conveyancer will ask the vendor particular questions about the property. In some states this is carried out prior to contracts becoming unconditional, and in others it is done after. The questions require vendors to disclose all known facts about their properties, including whether there is any non-approved building work or any environmental issues of which they are aware. Once again, you have no tasks at this stage, as these things will be done by your solicitor.

3. Arrange checks and inspections

Your conveyancer will usually make the necessary arrangements for the pest and building inspections to be done, unless you have a preference for who carries these out. Your conveyancer will also check to see if there are any outstanding arrears or land tax liabilities and make the necessary adjustments to rates which have been previously paid by the existing owner. If the property is strata titled, your conveyancer will examine the strata inspection report.

4. Act for you in the mortgage

Generally your conveyancer will receive and explain your mortgage documents to you. If you are using a broker, usually the broker can fulfil this role at no extra cost. A conveyancer may add an extra charge for this service, so be sure to ask about this and request that the bank sends the documents straight to you rather than through your solicitor. Of course, if you feel you need legal advice with regard to the mortgage, pay the extra fee and have it explained by a lawyer.

5. Preparation of transfer documents

Title transfer documents ensure that legal title to the property transfers to you, and that the land titles office now knows who the new owner is. These documents are also used by the government to determine whether you may be liable for land tax, although there is nothing on the title which declares whether the property is for investment purposes or not. Be sure that you are available to sign these documents as soon as they are ready so that settlement is not delayed.

Once settlement occurs, transfer documents must be lodged with the land titles office, so be sure that you ask for evidence that this has occurred. I have seen cases where absent-minded lawyers forgot to do this and months later the purchasers found that they were not registered as the legal owners of their new properties!

6. Pay the purchase stamp duty

The purchase stamp duty needs to be paid on the day of settlement or just before. Often conveyancers will ask for this cheque a few weeks prior to settlement, as it is easier for them to do it this way. However, in reality stamp duty can be paid simultaneously with settlement so, if you are using the equity in another property as your deposit, ensure that you make it clear to your conveyancer that you want loan proceeds to be used to pay the stamp duty.

Be sure to discuss this with your solicitors at the very first meeting so that they are aware of your requirements. The only time this does not apply is with an off-the-plan purchase. This is because there is a requirement that stamp duty be paid within a specified time of the contract for sale being signed. A standard settlement period is within this timeframe, but an extended settlement will often be outside of it. There is provision, however, to pay only a proportion of the required stamp duty if necessary.

7. Settlement

Settlement can be a major affair, particularly if you have a loan on the new property and are discharging existing loans at the same time. Basically settlement involves ensuring that the vendor's conveyancer is available to meet your conveyancer, and the lenders involved have provided the details to release any mortgages (held by you or the vendor), establish any new mortgages (for you) and hand over the title. This must take place all on the same day.

> **Tip!** A call to your new bank, your current bank and your conveyancer just to be sure they are all ready for settlement can't hurt.

I have seen settlement fall over for a number of reasons, mostly reasons which could not have been avoided by anything the investor could have done – but there is one notable exception.

Often investors who are discharging existing debts fail to keep up the repayments in the weeks leading up to settlement, resulting in the balance of those debts increasing. Should the amount of the new loan only just be enough to cover your purchase plus discharge of existing loans, there may not be enough money from the new loan to pay out the existing loan, and if this occurs the whole deal can fall over.

This is because banks usually cannot settle only part of a loan so they will not settle on any of it if there are not enough funds to settle the whole thing.

Be sure that you pay all loans right up until settlement date, and keep in touch with your solicitor and banks to ensure that you have completed all requirements. In addition, it would be useful to provide your conveyancer with the loan details document printed at the end of this section, as this will make it clear exactly what needs to be done on settlement.

The Conveyancing Process

8. Advice to authorities

Your solicitor or conveyancer should now advise local councils and water boards that the transfer has taken place. You have no tasks here except to check that this has been done.

> **Tip!** Go to **www.fairtrading.nsw.gov.au/realestaterenting/buyingselling/conveyancing.html** for a great document about conveyancing.

9. Acquit purchase

All too often conveyancers and solicitors do not adequately acquit the purchase to their clients. I have seen cases where, upon receiving the final figures, clients have discovered that something has been paid incorrectly, or overpaid or not paid at all.

As soon as you have made the decision to purchase, use the worksheet on buying costs, which you have completed in Step 3, along with the checklist at the end of this section to ensure that you meet all requirements and pay all costs when they fall due.

> **Tip!** Check off each and every transaction made on the day of settlement to be sure everything has been paid and the correct amounts have been applied.

Then ask the conveyancer to provide you with a comprehensive statement that details all disbursements and to whom they were paid. Check that this matches your estimates and, if not, ask why. Cross check the statements you receive from your discharging bank as well as the statements from your new bank and ensure that the amounts on those statements match the amounts paid to them by the conveyancer.

The Conveyancing Process

Dear Sir/Madam,

To assist with the efficient settlement of our new property, please find the following details:

1. Address of property to be purchased:

   ……………………………………………………

   ……………………………………………………

2. New loan to be established:

   Bank:…………………………………………………….

   Branch:…………………………………………….…….

   Total loan amount: …………………………………

3. Current loans requiring discharge:

   Bank:………………….   Branch:………………….

   Acc. #:…………………..

   Bank:………………….   Branch:………………….

   Acc. #:…………………..

4. Securities to be taken:

   Address:……………………………………………….

   Address:……………………………………………….

   Address:……………………………………………….

5. Disbursements to be made:

   Name:…………………..Amount: $………………..

   Name:…………………..Amount: $………………..

☑ Step 6 Checklist

- ☐ Solicitor/conveyancer chosen
- ☐ Details of vendor's solicitor/conveyancer given to your solicitor
- ☐ Contracts made unconditional
- ☐ Form regarding loan details provided to conveyancer
- ☐ Conveyancer advised of your method of paying stamp duty
- ☐ Details of all loans to be finalised provided
- ☐ Requisitions on title completed by conveyancer
- ☐ Transfer documents signed
- ☐ Stamp duty paid if applicable
- ☐ Property settled
- ☐ Local authorities notified
- ☐ Transfer documents lodged with land titles office
- ☐ Acquittal of purchase received from conveyancer
- ☐ Bank statements from discharging lender and new lender checked to conveyancer's statements and any discrepancies questioned

Step 7

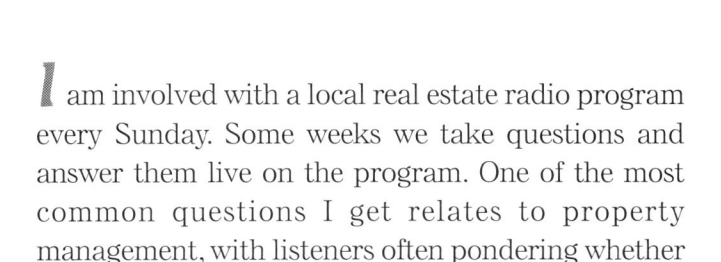

Property Management

I am involved with a local real estate radio program every Sunday. Some weeks we take questions and answer them live on the program. One of the most common questions I get relates to property management, with listeners often pondering whether they should carry out this management themselves.

I know a lot about computers, but I also know that I need experts to look after them for me. I know a lot about my swimming pool too, but there is nothing like having the pool technician give me advice and provide ongoing care to keep it looking good. As for my properties – well, I am a property owner not a property manager. The last thing I need is to have the hassles of managing my properties myself, especially now that I have ten of them. The money it costs me to have someone else do this, which by the way is tax deductible, is well worth it.

However, I have also heard stories of poor property managers, and I do understand the hesitation some people have to hand over the source of their future income to a company they know little about.

> **Tip!** Be sure you ask your property manager to advise you as soon as he or she receives notice of a tenant's departure. Then call the office every few days to make sure efforts are being made to get a new one.

Like every step discussed so far, getting your property well-managed is just another process you have to complete. You may have to do it a few times until it is right but the process is not really too difficult.

Choose the type of management

The property you buy will have one of several types of management. These are listed below, along with the questions you should ask and some methods of seeking out the right manager.

Standard residential management

This is where the property management section of a real estate agency, or a company which has property management as its exclusive activity, charges you a fee (usually a percentage of the rent collected) to oversee your property and to acquire and manage tenants for you. This is the most common form of property management and you must choose and supervise the manager yourself once the property has settled.

Choosing your residential manager

You must treat this process just as you would a job interview but with you as the employer. This is essentially what the arrangement is all about – you are hiring someone to do an important job for you.

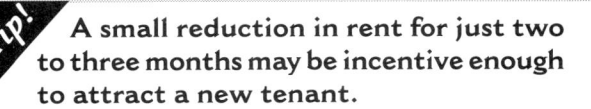

> **Tip!** A small reduction in rent for just two to three months may be incentive enough to attract a new tenant.

Where the property is close by, you can start by visiting a few local agencies and asking the list of questions below. Where the property is in another state you will have to let your fingers do the walking and either telephone a few agencies that you find in the *Yellow Pages* (www.yellowpages.com.au) or email any managers you can find on the internet.

Use www.google.com.au and type in 'property management' along with the location of your property at the search prompt.

The questions you must ask are:

1. How long have you been in property management?
2. How many properties do you currently manage?
3. How many staff are on hand to assist with property management?
4. In the event that no-one is in my property, what methods will you use to attract new tenants?
5. What is the full cost of management? Can you email me a list of every possible cost?
6. How many inspections per year do you carry out and at what cost?
7. How often are disbursements to the owner made? Can I have them made fortnightly and directly credited to my bank account?
8. What action do you take when a tenant is behind in rent?
9. How do you monitor tenant care of the premises?
10. Have you had any past complaints from other owners?
11. Who will manage my property when staff are on annual leave?
12. How many tenants on your books are currently in arrears?

Property Management

13. What is the vacancy rate currently across your entire rent roll?

14. Has your company been involved in any failed companies or ventures?

15. How many cases of serious tenant damage have you had in the past?

16. How do you screen tenants?

17. What can you do for me that another property manager cannot?

(Note: This list of questions is reproduced at the end of this section with spaces for you to record your answers.)

> **Tip!** **It takes the equivalent of 40 hours a year (or one working week) to manage one property. This means that a manager with more than 52 properties per staff member is overworked.**

Use your instincts to determine if the answers given suit you. You are looking for a manager who is not overworked (40 to 50 properties per staff member is ample), one with substantial experience and one who will come up with clever ideas when it comes to marketing your property. I always like the sound of someone who is prepared to offer me that little bit extra – perhaps a month free of management fees in order to prove themselves to me. I also like to make sure that the manager is amenable to me dropping the rent return in times of high vacancy – many are reluctant to do so, and while ten weeks vacancy may only mean a $120 total loss to them it could mean $1,200 to me!

What will it cost?

The cost of having your property tenanted will not be limited to just the management fee. The following are some expected costs:

1. A management fee, usually around 7% to 8% of the collected rent

2. Letting fees – usually the equivalent of one week's rent each time the property is let

3. Sundries – postage, photocopying, telephone calls, etc.

4. GST – not usually included in the quoted management fee

5. Water charges – in some states the owner pays the excess water as well as the basic rates

6. Cleaning costs – each time a tenant moves out

7. Advertising – to obtain new tenants

8. Inspection costs – to carry out each regular property inspection and inspections after each tenant has left

9. Pest control – if required

10. Pool care and maintenance

11. Repairs and maintenance

12. Lawn care.

Be sure to establish which of the management costs listed above are included in the base management fee and which are additional. Remember too that all things are negotiable – if you feel a charge is unreasonable, don't be afraid to say so and ask if it can be removed or reduced. Use the worksheet at the end of this section to ascertain the costs involved with each manager you interview for comparison.

How to terminate a poorly performing manager

When you sign a management agreement, be sure that the notice period required to terminate the manager is a short one. Many management agreements carry a ridiculous three-month termination period – far too long in the event that their performance is lacking and you wish to terminate.

Ensure that the period is no more than 14 days. Then watch your manager to be sure that you always know what is going on. If it does not perform as it has been contracted to, begin your search for a new one. Once you have found a successor, simply email or fax a termination letter and ask the new manager to go along and collect the keys for you.

Leasebacks

The property you purchase may come with an option for you to lease it back to an on-site operator. Typically this option will be available with serviced apartments, hotels and resorts, student accommodation and seniors' accommodation. In effect, the on-site operator becomes your tenant and pays the rent to you each week. It will hope that it can sublet your property for more than it is paying you and the difference will be its profit. Leasebacks often fail because of enthusiastic occupancy forecasting, and because the operator has no alternative source of income to support the rent payments in the event that occupancy is low.

Choosing your manager in a leaseback

Unfortunately, there is really no choice for you in these circumstances, usually because an on-site operator is in place long before the property you are buying is finished, or before you have effected your purchase.

Sometimes, however, you do have the choice as to whether you want to take part in the offered leaseback or not. If you choose not to, then the other option is to have a local property manager manage your property under a special arrangement for holiday or niche market occupancy. You may pay a higher management fee for an outside holiday property manager than you would for a standard residential letting service (usually up to around 12%)

but you are also going to be receiving all of the income the property attracts, not just the amount in the lease agreement offered by the on-site manager.

It can be hard to choose under these circumstances – an on-site manager may be better placed to attract occupancy, and the attraction of receiving a higher rent by having your property externally managed may be a zero sum game if an outside manager is just as unable to find frequent occupants for you.

> **Tip!** Ask the on-site operator to furnish you with a copy of its business plan and read it – you can tell a lot about a manager's preparedness from the quality of its business plan.

Before you proceed with a purchase that involves a leaseback, ask the following questions about the management:

1. What is your marketing plan for this property?
2. What is your experience with on-site property management?
3. What will be the actual income which I receive?
4. What additional costs will there be to pay?
5. How often will I receive rent payments?

6. How many properties does your company currently manage?

7. Have you had any past financial difficulties?

8. How are your other properties performing?

9. What has the vacancy rate been over the past 12 months?

What will it cost?

The cost of a leaseback is usually nothing, as you receive the amount stated in the lease agreement every week regardless of whether your property is being used or not. The property is most likely generating a much higher revenue than you are receiving, so this can be considered to be the cost.

Under a leaseback, all on-site costs such as repairs, maintenance and cleaning are generally covered by the tenant. In some cases a leaseback will state an actual percentage return (relating to the purchase price) which is net of all expenses – including your rates and utilities. All that is left for you to pay will be the loan interest.

If you choose to use an external property manager for your niche market property, you can expect the same costs as you would for your residential property management with a slightly higher management fee to cover the frequency of tenancy.

How to terminate an on-site manager

Essentially, if you have purchased a property with an on-site manager (whether it offers a leaseback or one of the other management arrangements to be covered next) this manager is retained by the body corporate of which you, as an owner, are a member. This means that, technically, the body corporate can vote to terminate a poorly performing manager. However, the contract by which it was originally hired will contain the conditions under which it can be terminated, and these conditions will be legally binding. This is why it is vital for you to be familiar with the terms of any contractual arrangement with any on-site manager *before* you proceed with the purchase of any property under management.

If you have a leaseback, ensure that you have a reasonable exit clause which allows you to terminate the agreement if necessary. Depending on the nature of the operator's agreement, the body corporate may have the power to terminate the entire operation if it has just cause. It will be up to the body corporate to then decide whether to retain a new on-site operator, or whether it would prefer all owners to seek their own external property managers.

Management agreements and management rights

Management rights usually involve a person or entity buying the rights to offer a letting service in a complex of properties. Usually the management rights contain the freehold over some property – perhaps an apartment plus the pool and reception.

> **Tip!** If your on-site manager does not have a written marketing plan you should ask it to write one.

A management agreement is an agreement between the body corporate and an operator for the operator to run a hotel or serviced apartment service for the owners. There is usually no option for the operator to own any part of the real estate in a management agreement.

Choosing a manager

Again you usually will not have any choice, as this arrangement is normally in place before you purchase a property. While you are doing your research, ensure that you find out as much as you can about these types of agreements if they are in place. You should ask the same questions as you would to the operator in a leaseback situation, but ensure you find out as much as you can about the true costs of the letting service being offered.

What will it cost?

On-site management of this nature normally has a fairly reasonable letting fee – around 7% to 8% of revenue received. The danger comes with the additional costs – there can be many and it is these costs that can result in little of the collected income being paid to you. Some of the additional costs you may be required to pay include:

1. Linen and laundry fees
2. Telephone charges
3. Workers' compensation
4. Public liability
5. Insurances
6. Pool chemicals
7. Gym maintenance
8. Motor vehicle care and maintenance where a courtesy bus is supplied.

The list goes on. Ensure you ask for a list of all of the possible costs.

Terminating a poorly performing manager

As with leasebacks, you will need to know what powers the body corporate has in the event that the manager does not perform well. Where the manager is under a management rights contract, you may have very little chance of being able to terminate it unless the body corporate can buy the management out, and this is most unlikely. Management agreements can be easier to terminate, but unless the body corporate is organised and has another manager ready to take over immediately, you could suffer loss of revenue during the notice period once the existing manager realises it will not be continuing.

> **Tip!** Never allow an agreement that stipulates more than 14 days notice to terminate a property manager of any standard residential property, and allow no more than 30 days in any other type of agreement.

It is vital that you read the sections on niche property management arrangements in *How to Maximise Your Property Portfolio* (from page 37 and page 109) for more comprehensive details about this type of arrangement.

Your responsibilities as a landlord

When you hand over management to someone else you do not also hand over your legal responsibilities. You have to ensure that you fulfil your duties and obligations so that you can provide your tenants with accommodation which they can enjoy. Basically your responsibilities are to:

1. Provide a fair, equitable and legal tenancy agreement, giving a copy to your tenant within 14 days of it being signed.

2. Consider all reasonable requests for tenancy and not discriminate.

3. Issue receipts promptly for any monies paid.

4. Only ask for rent in advance of two weeks for weekly rent payments, and one month for any rent payments required with less frequency than this.

5. Keep premises in good repair at all times.

6. Attend to urgent repairs immediately.

7. Attend to non-urgent repairs in a reasonable timeframe, but no more than 14 days from being made aware of the problem.

8. Ensure tenants always have keys.

9. Provide a clean and habitable premises.

10. Promptly repay any bond monies within 14 days of the tenant moving out.

How to Maximise Your Property Portfolio and *How to Create an Income for Life* include more comprehensive details of both landlord and tenant responsibilities.

Worksheet 7.1:
Questions for Residential Property Managers

1. How long have you been in property management? ………………………………..

2. How many properties do you currently manage? ……………………………………..

3. How many staff are on hand to assist with your management operation? ……………………

4. In the event that no-one is in my property, what methods will you use to attract tenants?

   …………………………………………………

   …………………………………………………

5. What is the full cost of management? Can you email me a list of every possible cost?

6. How many inspections per year do you carry out and at what cost? …………………………..

7. How often are disbursements to the owner made? Can I have them made fortnightly and directly credited to my bank account?

   ……………………………………………………

   ……………………………………………………

8. What action do you take when a tenant is behind in rent?

   ……………………………………………………

   ………………………………………… *cont'd...*

Worksheet 7.1 (cont'd): Questions for Residential Property Managers

9. How do you monitor tenant care of the premises?
   ....
   ....

10. Have you had any past complaints from other owners? ....
    ....

11. Who will manage my property when staff are on annual leave? ....

12. How many tenants on your books are currently in arrears? ....

13. What is the vacancy rate currently across your entire rent roll? ....

14. Has your company been involved in any failed companies or ventures? ....
    ....

15. How many cases of serious tenant damage have you had in the past? ....

16. How do you screen tenants?
    ....
    ....

17. What can you do for me that another property manager cannot? ....

Worksheet 7.2:
Questions to Ask where there is a Leaseback or Management Agreement

1. What is your marketing plan for this property? Can I see it? ....

2. What is your experience with on-site property management? ....
   ....

3. What will be the actual income that I receive?
   ....

4. Are there any other costs I will need to pay? What are they? ....
   ....
   ....

6. How often will I receive my rent payments?
   ....

7. How many properties does your company currently manage? ....

8. Have you had any past financial difficulties?
   ....

9. How are your other properties performing?
   ....

10. What has the vacancy rate been over the past 12 months? ....

Worksheet 7.3: Costs of Management

		Cost per annum
1.	Management fee	$..................
2.	Sundries	$..................
3.	Telephone	$..................
4.	Letting fee	$..................
5.	Inspections (x number per year)	$..................
6.	Advertising	$..................
7.	Cleaning fee	$..................
8.	Lawns	$..................
9.	Pool care	$..................
10.	Postage	$..................
11.	Linen/laundry	$..................
12.	Workers' compensation	$..................
13.	Pest control	$..................
14.	Motor vehicle	$..................
15.	GST	$..................
Total management costs		$..................

☑ *Step 7 Checklist*

☐ Reasonable weekly rent amount established

☐ List of potential local managers made

☐ Chosen manager interviewed – all questions asked and satisfied

☐ Where management is on-site under a leaseback or other agreement, all questions asked and research carried out (using questions from Worksheets 7.1 and 7.2 on pages 168 to 170)

☐ Financial viability of manager ascertained

☐ All associated costs established (use Worksheet 7.3 on page 171)

☐ Contract signed with chosen manager

☐ Lease agreement for new tenant signed and returned to tenant within 14 days

☐ Regular contact made with manager to ensure all is running smoothly

Step 8

Preparing for Tax

When tax time comes around, people seem to all rush about trying to lay their hands on the documents they need to send off to their accountants. If they have experienced a change in their personal circumstances, they may also be asking themselves whether the accountant they have will continue to be the best choice for them. Or, they may have just purchased their first investment and be on the lookout for the right person to prepare their tax returns.

It is my experience that there are few accountants who are exactly right for the job, so I have always found that it is good for me to know as much as I possibly can about the possible tax advantages that owning property as an investment can bring.

Then, at tax time, I can keep a watchful eye on my accountant to ensure he makes all of the possible claims.

By now you should have quite a number of items in your Property Portfolio File and some of these you may need for preparing a tax return. At this point it is vital that you read Chapter 10 of *How to Create an Income for Life*, Chapter 12 of *How to Make Your Money Last as Long as You Do* and Chapter 5 of *How to Maximise Your Property Portfolio* as these explain fully how the tax office will assess your claims, and what you can and cannot claim.

In this section we will look at what you have to do next and your responsibilities as a taxpayer.

Quantity surveyor's report

If you have purchased a property which you suspect will have on-paper deductions, the very first task you have to perform once you have settled on the property is to have a quantity surveyor's report prepared. This is because, although the tax office does allow you to make your own reasonable assumptions of the true value of the fixtures, fittings, furniture and original costs of construction, the realities are that you cannot hope to know the kinds of things you can claim, and you may miss out on some viable deductions.

In addition to this, you probably do not have the time, your property may be too far away and you have to provide compelling substantiating evidence as to why you make any assumptions you do make, so it is easier and probably more economically sound to simply retain the services of a reputable quantity surveyor.

The cost of having a depreciation schedule prepared is usually around $450. Your quantity surveyor will need to gain access to the property and may have some questions to ask you about its age, etc. Where you cannot provide the answers the surveyor can contact the council, but there is an added charge if this is necessary.

> **Tip!** Go to **www.depreciator.com.au** and **www.bmtassoc.com.au** for some great information on quantity surveyors' reports.

The depreciation schedule will provide you with a complete list of all the possible on-paper deductions you can make and details of the effective life of each item. A claimable item does not have to be new for it to be included on this report – a new effective life (based on current age and condition) will be given to each item, so you should be able to make a claim for virtually everything that is contained within the property.

What will I be able to claim?

If you go to www.ato.gov.au you can download a document called *Rental Properties*. This is an exceptionally good document which covers many of the details of how to claim, what to claim and what not to claim. It also looks at structuring and provides information on how the tax office will view your tenancy arrangements (that is, whose names will be on the titles and in what proportions you own each property).

Claims for the actual costs of owning a property fall into two main categories.

Capital costs

A capital cost is a cost you incur in the process of acquiring a property, selling a property or improving the capital value of a property. They are not costs which are required to be paid on an ongoing basis to allow the property to remain income producing.

A list of capital costs includes:

- Real estate agents' commissions
- Conveyancing costs such as search fees, solicitor's charges and sundries
- Government purchase stamp duties
- Building improvements of a capital nature not considered to be a repair

- Additions and renovations
- Driveways and pergolas
- Swimming pools.

Note that these are costs which occur either only once, or which add value to the property.

How do I claim capital costs?

You cannot claim a capital cost against earned income – that is, these costs cannot be claimed as a tax deduction on your yearly tax return.

You can, however, use the value of these costs to reduce any gain you make upon eventual sale, and so lessen the amount of capital gains tax you pay. In other words if you had, say, $12,000 worth of capital costs, then your taxable gain upon sale would be reduced by $12,000 and so you would pay less tax.

Revenue costs

A revenue cost is a cost you incur in the process of earning an income. These include:

- Costs of advertising for tenants
- Bank account keeping fees
- Body corporate fees (not including the portion attributed to a sinking fund)
- Cleaning
- Council rates

- Electricity and gas
- Gardening and lawn mowing
- Insurance
- Interest on loans
- Land tax
- Legal expenses
- Lease costs
- Loan interest
- Mortgage discharge fees
- Pest control
- Property agent's fees and commissions (management)
- Quantity surveyor's fees
- Repairs and maintenance
- Secretarial fees
- Security patrol fees
- Servicing costs
- Stationery and postage
- Telephone calls and rental of phone
- Tax-related expenses
- Travel and car expenses – to collect rent or inspect or maintain a property, but only where the sole purpose for the trip was property related
- Water charges.

Note that borrowing costs, such as establishment fees, title search fees, mortgage registration fees, mortgage broker fees, valuation fees, lender's mortgage insurance and loan stamp duty, are claimable over a five-year period or the term of the loan, whichever is less.

Note also that you must incur these charges to claim them – you may not make a claim for expenses on this list that were paid for by someone else, or for the full amount of expenses on a property which was not available for lease during the full claim period (for example a property which has some portion used for personal use, or a holiday property not available to tenants 52 weeks of the year. This does not mean it must be occupied 52 weeks of the year – it simply has to be *available* to be occupied).

How do I claim revenue costs?

Revenue costs may be claimed against any taxable income you make from any source in the year in which the claim is being made. You must keep all records, receipts and invoices which relate to the claimed expenses, and submit a 'Rental Property Schedule' (available as a download from the tax office website) for each property.

In essence, each dollar paid out is a dollar less on which you will pay tax. So, for example, if you earned $50,000 from employment and $10,000 from rent, but had expenses of $13,000, then you would only be liable to pay income tax on $47,000. Any tax you had paid on the $3,000 difference ($900 at 30% tax) would be sent back to you as a refund.

On-paper deductions

You may also be able to make a claim for the decline in value of depreciating assets. This effectively means that you can claim a tax deduction for the loss in value that all of the assets associated with your property incur. These claims are also divided into two categories – capital works deductions and fixtures, fittings and furniture deductions.

Capital works deductions

Depreciation deductions based on the original construction expenditure applying to capital works such as:

- A building or extension
- Alterations
- Structural improvements to the property, such as a pergola, patio, carport, driveway or retaining wall or fence.

Note that if you claim the depreciating costs of these items, you may not also claim the actual costs of acquisition against your capital gains tax liability, unless you add back any claimed depreciation amounts at the time of sale. See *How to Create an Income for Life* (page 174) for a complete explanation of the effect of adding back depreciation.

The actual expenditure that can be claimed includes:

- Architect's fees
- Engineer's fees
- Foundation excavations
- Payments to carpenters, bricklayers and other tradespeople
- Payments for the construction of retaining walls, fences and swimming pools.

Not included as claimable items are:

- The cost of the land
- The cost of clearing the land
- Permanent earthworks not integral to the construction
- Landscaping
- The builder's profit margin.

However, some of these things may form part of your cost base for capital gains tax purposes. The *Guide to Capital Gains Tax*, another ATO booklet (available from www.ato.gov.au), can provide more information about this. More about capital gains tax can also be found in each of my three prior books.

The amount of deduction depends on the type of construction and the date that the construction started. Table 8.1, below, is reproduced from *How to Maximise Your Property Portfolio*, and it summarises the relevant dates.

Table 8.1
Dates and Deduction Amounts

	None	2.5%	4%
Short-term or commercial			
before 22 Aug. 1979	✓		
22 Aug. 1979–19 Aug. 1982		✓	
20 July 1982–21 Aug. 1984			✓
22 Aug. 1984–15 Sep. 198			✓
Residential buildings			
before 18 July 1985	✓		
18 July 1985–15 Sep. 1987			✓
15 Sep. 1987–current		✓	
Tourist accommodation			
18 July 1985–15 Sep. 1987			✓
15 Sep. 1987–26 Feb. 1992		✓	
26 Feb. 1992–current			✓
Structural improvements			
After 26 Feb. 1992		✓	

Your quantity surveyor will establish the original construction cost of the property you have purchased, and you may then make claims according to the table above. It is important to note that you may only claim any balance of capital works deductions even if the prior owner has made no claims at all – so if the building is already, say, ten years old, then you can only claim the remaining 30 years.

How do I claim capital works deductions?

The original costs of the construction must be established once you have settled on the property. Where you are buying the property new, the builder or developer may be able to provide the details of the actual construction costs to you. Where you are purchasing an established property, and it qualifies for capital works deductions as per Table 8.1, the most efficient way for you to establish these costs will be through a quantity surveyor, and the fees for this service will be tax deductible.

Once established, include the amount of your claim on the Rental Property Schedule to be submitted with your tax return.

Fixtures, fittings and furniture

The value of each fixture, fitting and piece of furniture that is contained within your property may be depreciated over ATO accepted timeframes known as 'effective lives'. An example of some of the things upon which you can claim loss of value (and so a tax deduction) and their accepted effective lives are shown in Table 8.2 below.

Table 8.2
Items that Depreciate

Item	Effective life in years
Blinds	20
Carpets	10
Curtains	6.66
Electric clock	13.33
Electric heater	10
Furniture and fittings	13.33
Garbage disposal	6.66
Hot water installations	20
Lawn mowers	6.66
Floor coverings (lino)	10
Ovens/microwaves	6.66
Refrigerators	13.33
Stoves	20
Television receivers	10
Vacuum cleaners	10
Washing machines	6.66

> **Tip!** You may have a case for using a different effective life than that stated in Table 8.2. As long as you can substantiate your reasons for thinking an asset in your property should have a different figure, with evidence, then you may have a case.

In recent times some taxpayers have made an attempt to claim an item as a fixture, fitting or piece of furniture, when in fact the tax department considers it to be a 'part of the setting for income-producing activity'. Such items include:

- Built-in cupboards
- Door and window fittings
- Driveways and paths
- Electrical wiring
- Fencing and retaining walls
- Floor and wall tiles
- Garages and non-portable sheds
- In-ground swimming pools, saunas and spas
- Plumbing and gas fittings
- Reticulation piping
- Roller door shutters
- Roof top ventilators
- Security doors and screens permanently fixed

- Sinks, tubs and baths
- Wash basins and toilet bowls.

These items do, however, form part of the construction and will be included in the calculations for capital works deductions.

Calculating asset depreciation

You have two options by which you can claim the decreasing value of your assets. Both methods are explored fully in *How to Maximise your Property Portfolio* (page 85) and your accountant should be able to help you choose which is best for you. In a nutshell:

1. The diminishing value method

This method assumes that the decline in value is a constant proportion of the remaining value. The formula for determining the diminishing value method is:

$$\text{Base value} \times \frac{\text{Days held}}{365} \times \frac{150\%}{\text{Asset's effective life}}$$

As an example, the diminished value of carpet with an original value of $2,000 claimable for an entire year would be calculated as follows.

Year 1:

$$= \$2{,}000 \times \frac{365}{365} \times \frac{150\%}{10 \text{ years}}$$

$$= \$2{,}000 \times 1 \times 15\%$$

$$= \$300 \text{ (Year 1 claim)}$$

Year 2:

$$= \$1{,}700 \times \frac{365}{365} \times \frac{150\%}{10 \text{ years}}$$

$$= \$1{,}700 \times 1 \times 15\%$$

$$= \$255 \text{ (Year 2 claim)}$$

and so on.

2. *The prime cost method*

This method assumes that an asset loses value uniformly over time. The formula for determining the prime cost method is:

$$= \text{Asset's cost} \times \frac{\text{Days held}}{365} \times \frac{100\%}{\text{Asset's effective life}}$$

As an example, the reduction in value of the same carpet would be calculated as follows.

Year 1:

$$= \$2{,}000 \times \frac{365}{365} \times \frac{100\%}{10 \text{ years}}$$

$$= \$2{,}000 \times 1 \times 10\%$$

$$= \$200$$

Year 2:

$$= \$2{,}000 \times \frac{365}{365} \times \frac{100\%}{10 \text{ years}}$$

$$= \$2{,}000 \times 1 \times 10\%$$

$$= \$200$$

And so on until the full original cost has been totally written off.

> **Tip!** The diminishing value method allows for a higher claim in the early years and a lower one in the later years. Where you need more deductions early on to make a property positive cashflow, and you know you can repay debt quickly to assist in reducing the costs and so keep the property positive cash flow as your deductions begin to run out, then choose the diminishing value method.

You are free to choose whichever method you like but, once chosen, you must stick with one method for the life of the claim. The free Destiny Finsoft calculator provides automatic calculations for both of these methods.

Other claims

Items under $300 have an immediate claim available in the year in which they were purchased or acquired. These include items such as crockery, cutlery, bedding, linen, etc.

You may also allocate low-cost assets (items which are low-cost to purchase) and low-value assets (assets with a low value at the beginning of the period, and this may include items which have now been written down low enough in value) to a 'low-value pool'.

In essence this means that any item with a cost, an adjusted value or a written down value under $1,000 may be allocated to this pool, and the total value of the pool is then depreciated at a diminishing value rate of 37.5%. Once you choose to create a low-value pool you must allocate all low-cost and low-value assets in that year and in subsequent years to this pool.

I suggest that you leave this job up to your accountant, but be sure he or she knows about low-value pooling and can arrange this for you.

Structuring your purchase

In Step 4, we briefly looked at how to choose the type of tenancy and in whose name the property should be purchased. Detailed examples were given on page 188 of *How to Create an Income for Life* and page 104 of *How to Maximise Your Property Portfolio* to show the impact of choosing the wrong structure at the outset. The following is a summary of the types of structures you can choose.

Joint names or single names?

Whether you choose to buy your property in two names or just one name depends on who needs the tax advantages the most. To ascertain this, you need to have done some rough calculations to establish what type of cash flow you have on the property.

If the property is negatively geared, and you expect this to remain so for a long time, you will need to buy the property in the name of the highest income earner as this will maximise your tax advantages. Where both parties earn similar incomes, and you expect this to continue, buy in joint names.

Where the property is positively geared, and there are no on-paper deductions available to reduce the income, then buy the property in the lower income earner's name. Where both parties earn similar incomes and you expect this to continue then buy in joint names.

> **Tip!** If you think that one party may be about to have a change in income or perhaps leave the workforce, be sure to take this into consideration when choosing in whose name you buy.

Where the property is positive cash flow because of the deductions, then you must buy in the names of the person in the highest tax bracket. This is because the higher the tax bracket, the more tax is available to get back. Where both parties earn similar incomes and you expect this to continue, buy in joint names.

It is vital that you assess the property past year one. Note that the table at the end of Step 2 (page 55) gives some sample depreciation figures for properties of nominated amounts, and the accompanying notes show you how you can adjust these. They also point out how depreciation is likely to change over time and how, due to the effect of a low-value pool and the 100% write-off of items under $300, your on-paper claims in the second and subsequent years may be less than they are in year one.

A property showing a positive cash flow in year one may not do so in year two and beyond unless you have paid off some of the debt or increased your rent return. So, assess the cash flows of the property carefully, consider how much debt you may be able to eliminate each year, and choose whose name to buy the property in according to a long-term view.

Joint tenants or tenants in common?

There are two main factors on which to base this decision.

Firstly, how would you like your asset to be distributed in the event of your death? If you want the other owner(s) to automatically receive your share, then buy in joint names, as this will allow your share of this asset to fall outside your estate, so it cannot be included in your will. If you want to leave your share to someone else, then buy as tenants in common as this will allow you to include your investment in your will.

A couple on equal incomes would usually only choose a tenants in common arrangement if they did not want to leave property to each other.

> **Tip!** Destiny Finsoft allows you to make calculations using one name or both, to assess the best option for you to use.

The second reason is for tax purposes. Joint tenants equally share income and expenses. The only exception to this rule is loan interest in the event that one party borrows money to buy their share. In this case, that one party may attribute all of the interest on the loan to his or her personal circumstances, while income and expenses are equally split. However, the tax department would not accept one party claiming interest on a loan amount which is equal to the entire value of the property!

If you wish to divide income and expenses unequally, then you must buy as tenants in common and specify on the title deed the percentage share each person owns. This percentage share then becomes the basis for splitting both income and expenses – you cannot choose a different split just because one party earns more income (from other sources) in a particular year than the other party.

Land tax

You become liable to pay land tax when the land value of your property holdings (not including the family home) in a particular state exceeds a certain value. Once this happens you are required to declare the amounts you are liable for and pay this tax. Land tax is a tax-deductible revenue cost.

Each state has a different threshold for levying land tax, and each year this threshold increases according to the consumer price index (CPI). At present the land tax in New South Wales starts after a value of $317,000 and this is similar in other states.

Remember that land tax is applied to the value of the land component only, the value of which is determined by the valuer general. These determinations are often much lower than the current market values.

> **Tip!** You can minimise land tax by ensuring that you buy in a number of different states. In addition, the land component of units is usually very low, so include a few units, townhouses or duplexes in your purchases.

Prepaying interest and expenses

You are allowed to prepay up to 12 months of interest expenses and other expenses providing the period you are claiming ends on or before June 30 the following year. You can then claim this as an immediate deduction. Investors would choose to do this where they had made a profit from positive gearing in year one but expected that this situation could change in the future, or if they expected income from employment to dramatically decrease, forcing them into a lower tax bracket for the following year.

Before prepaying any expenses, do be sure that there really is a long-term benefit for you.

Keeping records

The tax office requires that you keep accurate records regarding your income and expenses.

You may be asked to provide records which show:

- The exact date an asset was acquired
- The exact date an asset was disposed of and the sale price
- Any amount which may form part of a cost base, such as renovation and improvement costs
- Records relating to income received
- Records relating to costs incurred
- Quantity surveyor's reports.

Keep all rent receipts (statements from your property manager), purchase receipts and services invoices. Use the 'Assets Register' at the end of this section to keep an accurate record of any assets acquired or sold after the date that your depreciation report is prepared.

Getting the tax back now!

Positive cash flow property which is the result of on-paper claims generally presents a loss situation until you get your tax back. The tax you get back may make up this loss and give you extra money in your pocket as well.

If you wait until the end of the year to make your claims, you will need to fund any loss in the meantime. The net result of funding this loss is that you have less cash available in the short term to reduce your debt and so save interest on your loan. Some people like to get their tax back all in one lump sum. The problem is that the tax office will not pay you interest on your money which, in effect, it has held for up to 12 months.

As soon as you settle on your new property, you should telephone the tax office and ask for it to send you a Request to Vary Taxation form. This is a very simple form on which you make estimates of your income, expenses and on-paper deductions. If this estimate shows a loss, the tax office will write to your employer and adjust the amount of tax which needs to be deducted from your pay each pay period. This way you get the tax breaks each time you are paid. You can then use this money (which you did not need before anyway) as extra repayments into any debt you have (remember, personal debt first, investment debt next). You will not only offset interest but you will more rapidly reduce your debt and so gain equity for faster leveraging.

Be sure to slightly underestimate your expenses and overestimate your income. This builds in a margin to ensure you are not wrong and will not have any penalties to pay to the tax office at the end of the financial year.

Worksheet 8.1: Assets Register

Assets acquired

Date of Acquisition	Asset Description	Cost/Value

Assets disposed of

Date of Disposal	Asset Description	Sale Price

☑ Step 8 Checklist

- ☐ Establish the age of the property if it is not new
- ☐ Obtain quantity surveyor's report
- ☐ Establish original costs from developer or builder if applicable
- ☐ Start an asset register (see Worksheet 8.1, page 197)
- ☐ Record any sale or purchase of assets
- ☐ Ask your accountant about a low-value pool
- ☐ Establish whether to use the prime cost or diminishing value method for calculating depreciation
- ☐ Establish borrowing costs so that they can be claimed over a five-year period
- ☐ Ascertain if land tax will apply
- ☐ Ensure property structure and tenancy arrangements are correct
- ☐ Keep all receipts and records in your Property Portfolio File
- ☐ Order a Request to Vary form from the tax office
- ☐ Complete Request to Vary form and lodge immediately

Step 9

Selling Your Property

I firmly support a buy and hold strategy for property. I believe that the best results are obtained by ensuring that you buy, using all of the criteria outlined in this book, and then not only hold for the long term, but keep your property so that you can have a steady flow of income once you have chosen to leave the paid workforce.

This way you also enjoy the leveraging benefits that capital growth can bring without suffering the drawbacks of paying capital gains tax.

However, there are several situations in which you may consider selling, so you will need to understand the selling process.

Why sell?

How to Maximise Your Property Portfolio (page 54) covered some of the occasions on which you might have to sell. You might also have some personal reasons for making such a decision. Some of the more common reasons include:

▸ Your property has a vacancy rate of more than eight weeks a year. You cannot see this improving and your cash flows are too negative.

▸ The property is stagnant or going backwards in value and cash flow is very low or negative.

▸ The property is in an area where you are having constant problems – e.g. vandalism or unsavoury tenants – and you cannot see this changing in the future.

▸ The area has enjoyed a significant growth in value (a large boom). You feel that the boom is over, and that keeping this property is preventing you (from a borrowing point of view) from accessing other property in potentially high-growth areas.

▸ You have left the paid workforce and would like to realise some of the equity you have in your portfolio to either use as cash or to invest into other assets.

Selling Your Property

Whatever the reason, you will not only need to know about the processes involved in selling, but also the implications from a capital gains tax perspective, before you can be sure you are doing the right thing.

Capital gains tax

Any gain realised on the sale of a property which was used for income-producing purposes, and purchased after 19 September 1985, will incur capital gains tax as per the following.

For properties purchased after 19 September 1985 and before 21 September 1999:

Sale price

Minus Indexed purchase price (according to tax office rates – see www.ato.gov.au)

Plus Claimed special building write-off for period held

Minus Original costs to buy and improve (see Step 8, Capital Costs)

Equals Capital gain

Multiplied by Marginal rate of tax

Equals Capital gains tax liability

For properties purchased after 21 September 1999 and held more than 12 months:

Sale price

Minus Full purchase price

Plus Claimed special building write-off for period held

Minus Original costs to buy and improve (see Step 8, Capital Costs)

Equals Capital gain

Divided by Two

Multiplied by Marginal rate of tax

Equals Capital gains tax liability

For properties purchased after 21 September 1999 and held less than 12 months:

Sale price

Minus Full purchase price

Plus Claimed special building write-off for period held

Minus Original costs to buy and improve (see Step 8, Capital Costs)

Equals Capital gain

Multiplied by Marginal rate of tax

Equals Capital gains tax liability

Note: If you purchased prior to 21 September 1999 then you have the choice as to which of these formulas you use.

Avoiding capital gains tax

The only reliable way to avoid paying capital gains tax is to retain your property. This way you will not realise a gain (in your hands as profit) and so cannot be taxed.

There is no truth to the rumour that you can move into your investment property for a time and so avoid this tax, otherwise we would all be doing it. If you do live in a property which at some time earns an income for you, you must determine the period of time that the property was income producing and so pay tax on a pro rata basis. For example, if you owned a property for two years and lived in it for six months, you must declare three quarters of your gain (at the rates determined by the appropriate formula) for capital gains tax purposes.

You can, however, minimise the amount of tax that you do pay by being careful when you liquidate property. Choose a time to sell when your income is at its lowest – perhaps the first year you retire. *How to Maximise Your Property Portfolio* shows you how staggering the sale of property over several years can dramatically reduce the amount of tax you pay. Of course, if you happen to have capital losses through the sale of other assets, you can offset these against any future gains you make.

Capital losses

You cannot claim a capital loss against other income in your tax return. You may only use capital losses to offset capital gains. In the event that you do incur a capital loss from the sale of any asset, and you have no capital gains against which to write-off these losses, you may carry them forward and write them off against future capital gains.

The selling process

1. Choose your method of sale

If you have decided you would like to sell, you must choose your method of sale. Where the property is in close proximity to where you live, you may choose to undertake this task on your own. However, do be aware of the drawbacks – you must be available to show people the property whenever they would like to see it, you must have access to a reasonably wide net for advertising and you need to have some selling skills.

Generally, selling is a job to be left to the professionals and, in many cases, your property is not going to be close enough for you to carry out

Selling Your Property

this job efficiently. You will need an experienced real estate agent who can fulfil the following tasks:

- Give a fair indication of the real price your property can fetch
- Provide a fair assessment of the best way to sell your property, including advice on whether an auction would be a suitable course for you
- Show you that he or she understands how to effectively advertise and promote your property
- Access a large number of potential buyers
- Ensure that your security needs are observed at all times
- Negotiate the best price for you
- Present all offers to you for consideration
- Ensure you are aware of all of your obligations in the sale
- See you through to settlement and remain in communication with you at all times.

Just as it was necessary for you to interview potential property managers, your job of selecting the right agent to sell for you is one which requires you to ask a number of questions and use your instincts as to who you feel can perform this job honestly and ethically.

You should ask the following questions:

1. What is a fair price for the property? What do you base this on?
2. What is your commission rate?
3. Do I have to pay for anything else – such as advertising, marketing, etc.?
4. How will you market the home?
5. Who will accompany prospective purchasers on inspections?
6. After what period of time without a sale will you take further action?
7. What kind of action will you take?
8. How quickly will you present offers to us?
9. What is your track record?
10. What can you do for me that another agent cannot?

Add to this list any other questions you can think of and be sure to ask them of any agent to whom you speak.

2. Choose the type of selling agreement

a. Exclusive agency agreement

This is where you appoint one real estate agent to undertake the task of selling the property. No other agent is allowed to advertise it and you are exclusively listed with just one agent. You will be able to build a good rapport with this person and hopefully he or she will provide a 100% effort for you and a small number of other exclusive listings.

b. General listing/open agency

This is where a number of agents try to sell your property, with a commission paid to whoever ultimately sells it. This type of listing is not usually given the same time and effort as an exclusive agreement and you may end up paying extra in advertising costs, etc.

c. Multi-listing

You will deal with one agent who has access to a whole network through a multi-listing agreement. Usually the commission you pay will be split between the agency which has the listing and the agent who ultimately sells the property.

3. Preparation of contracts

Firstly determine the list of fixtures and fittings to be included in the sale, and ensure you write these things on the contract. All states have different requirements for the preparation of sale contracts, so be sure to review Step 4 and to check all of the contract requirements for the relevant state.

4. Preparing the property

If you have tenants, they must be advised that the property is on the market. Although it is law for you to give seven days notice of an inspection to a tenant, it is also law that you only need to provide 24 hours notice of a visit by a prospective buyer.

Most states allow an 'open house' method of presentation, where your house is open for public inspection during set hours, once a week. Of course, buyers can be shown through the house at times other than this at your discretion. Where you have tenants, they may not be happy about you holding too many public inspections, and you cannot be sure they will always present the home in the manner you would wish, so think carefully before choosing to do this.

As a landlord who will probably not be present for the sale process, you can have little impact on how the home is presented for sale. However, ensure that your property manager conducts a good inspection beforehand, so that you can perform any required repairs and otherwise attend to any problems.

5. Negotiation and accepting an offer

Step 4 covers the way a property is negotiated upon in each state. Note that although your purchaser will pay a 10% deposit, this is generally not available for your use unless the purchaser specifically agrees to it being released. Funds will not become available until the settlement, which usually occurs within 42 days of an unconditional contract being put in place.

What will it cost?

The Free Destiny Finsoft program includes a buying and selling worksheet which you can use to automatically calculate the true costs of selling. If you want to make a manual list, be sure to include:

- Sales commissions
- Land tax certificate
- Conveyancing costs
- Searches
- Council certificates
- Costs to repair the property
- Advertising costs
- Auction costs
- Loan discharge fees
- De-registration of mortgages
- Loan interest up to settlement
- Settlement charges (from the discharging bank)
- Cleaning costs
- Other.

If you are very thorough with your list, you can ascertain the true net amount you expect to receive from the sale and you will not have any nasty surprises.

What next?

If you have sold to enable you to buy more property, get straight back into it. This country is full of people who have liquidated their one and only investment property to provide funds for a holiday or new car, and years later they are in exactly the same position they were in before they ever bought the property.

Be sure to use the funds you realise to either buy more property, or to buy other growth and income producing assets. You should also make sure you don't forget to keep accurate records about your sale price, and net receipts, so that you can provide these to your accountant and ensure that your capital gains tax liabilities are fulfilled.

Worksheet 9.1: Selling Costs

Sale Costs

Sales commissions	
Land tax certificate	
Conveyancing costs	
Searches	
Council certificates	
Costs to repair property	
Advertising costs	
Auction costs	
Total	$

Lender Costs

Loan discharge fees	
De-registration of mortgages	
Loan interest up to settlement	
Settlement charges (by discharging bank)	
Total	$

cont'd...

Worksheet 9.1 (cont'd): Selling Costs

Other Costs

Cleaning costs	
Other	
Total	$

Total costs	$
Sale price	$
Net to be received	$
Less applicable cost base (see 'Capital Gains Tax' page 201)	$
Assessable gain (divide by two if applicable)	$
Tax to be paid (at your marginal rate of tax)	$
Net profit to you	$

☑ Step 9 Checklist

- ☐ Ascertain the reason for selling
- ☐ Determine your applicable method of calculating capital gains tax
- ☐ If it was not used as an investment property 100% of the time, ascertain the period in which the property was income-producing
- ☐ Establish any prior capital losses
- ☐ Choose a method of sale – private or professional
- ☐ Type of selling agreement chosen – exclusive, general, multi-listing
- ☐ Contracts prepared
- ☐ Property prepared and tenants advised
- ☐ Decide whether to make the property open for public inspections
- ☐ Selling worksheet used
- ☐ Capital gains liability established and accountant advised

Step 10

A Few Extra Insights

Even after you have settled on your new property there are always a few final traps you need to be aware of and so I have a few final bits and pieces of information to offer. These insights are not crucial to the buying process, but are tips which may assist you with growing your portfolio and stop you from getting into any trouble.

My own home would make a great investment property

Many investors come to me with this statement. Perhaps it would. Whether or not it makes a sound financial choice is another matter.

People often want to move from a house that they have occupied for some years, keep it as an investment, raise a new debt and build their dream home to live in. The following advice should be heeded:

1. Where the property you are moving from has a small, or no, debt, and you are raising a larger debt for the new owner-occupied home, this is a poor choice. You will end up with an income on the house you moved out of with little debt available to write off, and a large non-taxable debt on the house you live in.

    Far better to sell your current house, use the proceeds and raise a small debt for the new owner occupied home, then use the equity in that house to raise a debt for 100% of the purchase price of a new investment property (and probably one that has better investment potential anyway).

2. Where you still have a large debt on the house you are moving from, this may work, but please do the calculations to be sure.

Ask yourself why you want to keep the house you are moving out of anyway. If it is because you love it, then you will not be able to stand watching someone else treat it differently than you would yourself. Ask yourself why you are moving if you love it so much.

Landlord's insurance

You must have landlord's insurance on every investment property you own. There are many types and not all of them are good. Ensure the policy you are looking at covers:

- Building and contents
- Public liability
- Loss of rent (through tenant damage)
- Repair of tenant damage
- Recovery of unpaid rent.

Do I have to register for GST?

If you are not 'carrying on the business of rental properties' then you do not have to register for GST. You will only be carrying on this type of business if it is all you do and if you have substantial holdings in property. If this is so, the way you earn and claim income and expenses will also be different.

If you get to the point where you have a lot of properties and you think you may benefit from claiming GST input credits then you may wish to register for GST. Bear in mind that once you do this you will also have to complete a regular Business Activity Statement (BAS) and fulfil other responsibilities.

Property seminars

I feel quite vindicated that all of my warnings about expensive property seminars this year proved true when a large group headed by one very enthusiastic spruiker was brought down. I do not feel so good about the poor people of whom he took shameful advantage, many of whom spent life savings on his promises.

Things never change. You can learn just as much spending $100 on a couple of good books as you can spending $10,000 on the promise of fabulous wealth by someone who creates their own fortune by hoodwinking you.

Rent or buy?

Should you save up to buy a house in which to live, or buy a house as an investment and rent yourself?

This depends on how you feel about renting, and on where you want to live. If you want to live in an area that is out of your price range at present, and it will take many more years of renting until you finally save enough (by which time the prices in the area will have gone up and you may still be unable to afford it anyway!) then consider buying one or two cheap properties as an investment, ensuring they are positive cash flow (and so pay for themselves) and use the extra cash flow and what you are currently saving to continue to save. This way, not only are you saving a deposit, but you have property which is currently accessing capital gain and is, in effect, adding to your savings. You can keep buying more property like this until the time comes that your savings plus your growing equity is enough for a deposit, and you can then leverage this back into the house you want to buy to live in.

If you want to live in an area you feel you can fairly quickly save for, then go for the owner occupied house. Pay as much off as quickly as you can, then leverage into an investment property as soon as you are able.

I don't have the internet

Then be sure to have it connected. You cannot possibly hope to succeed in today's property market if you do not have access to the latest technology. For internet access you only need a small and not terribly flash computer and these days some dial up service providers have access from just $10 a month. Or go to the library or an internet café. But please, do not use this as an excuse not to start. Get connected and do it today!

Can I make a negatively geared property positive?

Probably not, unless you have never had a quantity surveyor's report done. In this case it is possible, if there are things you have been missing. In this event, get one done quickly and ensure you put in a retrospective claim for unclaimed expenses to the tax office.

Some people consider buying furniture to add on-paper claims to their property. This may work but having furniture may be a drawback for potential tenants unless your property is in an area with a known itinerant population.

If you have a few positive cash flow properties, do not let this be an excuse to buy a negatively geared property which you have secretly had your eye on.

If you have a negatively geared property, see page 54 of *How to Maximise Your Property Portfolio* to establish if you should sell it or not. Otherwise run out and buy a few positive cash flow properties to make up for the weekly loss!

Note from the Author

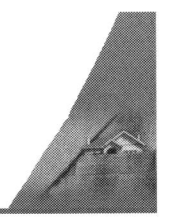

I love buying property and I love writing even more. One day I am going to write an epic novel in the style of *War and Peace*, but for now I am satisfied that I have the chance to share the knowledge I continue to acquire about property through my love of writing.

The year 2003 was a tough one for me with the death of both my father and a good friend. Sometimes it takes major events like these to send us looking for more answers. Well, I haven't found mine yet, but I am thankful for the caring nature of so many of my readers who have responded so warmly to my newsletters and who sent their condolences for my losses.

Most of all I love to hear about the successes of the people who read my books – if you have a story to tell please write to me about it. There is nothing more rewarding than to hear of how someone's life may have changed, even just a tiny bit, because they read something they liked and then used this new information to help themselves.

You now have the process which should make buying positive cash flow property so much easier and so much less stressful. Be sure to use all of the worksheets, and don't skip any steps. Soon you will be the proud owner of property which should perform well for you for years to come.

Be sure to email me and let me know how you are going and never stop striving to be the very best you can be. Don't listen to the knockers – do what you feel in your heart is right. Human instinct is a marvellous thing and if you just trust yours you will achieve great things.

One day I am going to plan a big party in every state to which I am going to invite all of those experienced and new positive cash flow property investors. That way we can have a lovely time congratulating each other on how clever we have all been.

Happy investing!

Glossary

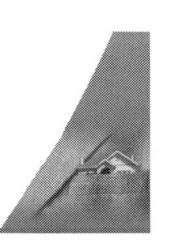

ASIC: Australian Securities and Investments Commission.

Body corporate: An owners' committee with owners volunteering for positions. These are in place to manage funds collected to maintain common property in strata titled properties.

Bond: An amount of money paid by a tenant and held in trust to cover any damage at the end of a rental period.

Borrower: A party to a loan – the person borrowing the funds.

Business plan: A document outlining the future plans of a business and projecting income and expenses for the planned period.

Capital costs: Costs incurred when purchasing a property as well as those paid for structural improvements.

Capital gain: The profit made on an investment.

Capital loss: The loss made on an investment.

Certificate of title: Legal proof of ownership of a property, carrying the owner's name and other information.

Commission (real estate): Fee payable to a real estate agent (or other salesperson) for selling a property by the person authorising the sale. Usually a percentage of the sale price, or can be a set fee where a relationship between the developer and salesperson exists.

Common property: Areas in strata-titled properties shared and maintained by all owners.

Community titled: A title whereby you own the land on which your house sits and you share the title to all other land around it with other people.

Consumer price index (CPI): A fixed, weighted price index that relates to household expenditure on retail goods and services and other items such as housing, government charges and consumer credit charges.

Contract Note: The document completed on agreeing to a final purchase price. It contains details of the conditions of the Contract of Sale (used in Victoria only).

Glossary

Contract of sale: Written agreement setting out the terms and conditions of a property sale.

Conveyancing: Legal process of transferring the ownership of a property from one person to another. Can be carried out by either a property solicitor, a conveyancer or a settlement agent.

Deposit: Usually 5% to 10% of the purchase price of a property placed in trust upon exchange or signing of the contract.

Deposit bond: An insurance policy guaranteeing a purchaser's deposit in the event of a contract default.

Depreciation: Where the original cost of an item is progressively written off over its effective life.

Developer: The person providing the funds (personal or borrowed) and taking the risk for building a property for sale.

Equity: The difference between what you owe and what you own of a property.

Fittings and fixtures: Items such as baths, stoves, lights and other fittings, kitchen, linen or storage cupboards and wardrobes. Fittings are not normally included in a contract if they can be removed without causing damage.

Fixed-rate loans: Loans with an interest rate that remains the same for a pre-agreed term.

Forecast: Assumptions made (often on paper by developers) about the future growth and income earning potential of an investment, based on historical performance and projected future events.

Gazumping: Where the vendor accepts an offer from another buyer after agreeing to your price, and this other buyer manages to have his or her contract become unconditional before yours.

Gross income: Income earned before tax and any costs.

Guarantor: A party to a loan who is not a borrower. A guarantor provides a guarantee for the debt to be paid in the event that the borrower defaults. Often a guarantor provides security for a debt for someone else.

Interest: The sum charged by the lender, calculated on the outstanding balance of borrowings, in deference to having supplied you with funds.

Interest-only loans: A loan on which only the interest is paid periodically and the principal is paid at the end of the term.

Investment: The purchase of a security with the ultimate goal of producing capital gain or an income.

Joint tenants: Joint tenancy is the equal holding of property by two or more persons. When one party dies, the remaining tenants share the portion owned by the deceased.

Land tax: Value-based levy applied to some property. Varies from state to state.

Landlord: The owner of an investment property.

Glossary

Lease: A document granting possession of a property for a given period without conferring ownership. The lease document specifies the terms and conditions of occupancy by the tenant.

Leverage: To utilise the growth in any one investment vehicle to invest into more vehicles.

Line of credit: An interest-only mortgage that has a credit limit and into which you can deposit and withdraw funds at will, up to this limit.

Loan to valuation ratio (LVR): The percentage of your loan amount as a total value of its security.

Mine subsidence: Areas where the land is prone to slip due to previous or current mining. A certificate can be issued attesting to a property's stability in a mine subsidence area.

Mortgage: Legal agreement on the terms and conditions of a loan for the purpose of buying real estate, whereby the person offering the mortgage takes security over the property.

Negative gearing: The writing off of investment property losses where a negative cash flow results – that is, expenses exceed income.

Net income: In-hand income after tax and costs.

Net profit: Remaining funds left after all costs are paid.

Niche market property: Property that is zoned residential but provided for specific markets – such as tourism, retirement or student.

Occupancy: Period that a tenant occupies a property.

On-paper deductions: Tax claimable items which do not have a relative cash outlay.

On-site management: Care and letting of premises carried out by a manager who lives at the site.

Owner-occupied: Property in which the owners reside. In other words, non-income-producing property.

Positive cash flow: The net positive income earned on a property after adding rent plus tax breaks and deducting actual property costs.

Positive gearing: Where income on an investment property exceeds expenses and tax must be paid on the gain.

Principal: The original amount of money that has been borrowed not considering accruing interest.

Repayment: The amount required by a lender to repay a loan, including its interest, within a set period of time.

Revenue costs: Costs incurred to earn income on an investment property.

Risk profile: An outline of the level of risk with which investors are comfortable. Obtained according to their responses to questions on how they feel about investing and their personal investing choices.

Security: Property offered to the mortgagee in return for a loan.

Settlement: Completion of sale (or advancing of a loan) when the balance of a contract price is paid to the vendor and the buyer is legally entitled to take possession of the property.

Special building write-off: The amount of depreciation that can be claimed on the construction costs of an investment property.

Stamp duty: A state government tax imposed on the sale of real estate.

Strata title: Most commonly used for flats and units, this title gives you ownership of a small piece of a larger property and includes common property.

Tax: An amount of money paid to the government as a percentage of each dollar earned.

Tax benefits: Any allowable item which reduces the amount of tax you must pay.

Taxable income: Income on which tax is paid after allowable deductions have been considered.

Tenancy in common: The holding of property by two or more persons, with either equal shares or unequal shares. If one person dies, the property is dealt with in accordance with the will.

Tenant: Either the person signing a lease to occupy premises or the description of a party to a property title.

Term: The time span of a loan.

Torrens title: Basic freehold title.

Vacancy: Period of time a property is without a tenant.

Valuation: Assessment of the value of a property given in a written report by a registered valuer.

Valuer: A person licensed to give an estimation of the value of property.

Variable rate loan: A home loan for which the interest rate changes as the money market changes.

Vendor: Person offering a property for sale.

Index

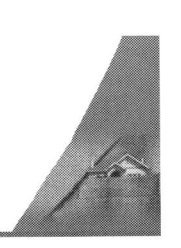

agent's commissions 176
asset depreciation
   — calculating, diminishing value method 186
   — calculating, prime cost method 187
assets register 195, 197
auctions 36-37, 205
Australian Bureau of Statistics (ABS) 84
Australian Securities and Investments Commission (ASIC) 18
Australian Taxation Office (ATO) 176, 179, 181, 183, 196, 210

banks 17-22 (*see also* 'lenders' *and* 'loan applications')

Baynet (*see* 'Credit Advantage Limited')
body corporate 72
   — fees 67, 177
building depreciation 44, 77
building inspections 66, 72, 145
Business Activity Statements (BAS) 217
buyers' advocates 38-39, 61

calculating cash flow 43-45
capital cities 4
capital costs 176
capital gains tax 49, 199, 201-204
   — capital losses 204
capital works deductions 180, 183

commercial property 47, 49
comparative pricing 91
consumer price index (CPI) 4, 6, 193
contracts
— signing the contract 96-102
— state-by-state requirements 96-102, 107
conveyancing costs 65, 143-150, 176
cooling off periods 99
Credit Advantage Limited (CAL) 126

debt reduction 10
debt servicing ratio 18-22, 24
demographics 76
deposits 104-105
— deposit bonds 104
depreciation 42, 44
— depreciation schedule 42, 174-175
— fixtures, fitting and furniture 183-184
— low-cost items 189-190
— sample depreciation figures 55
Destiny Financial Solutions 13
Destiny Finsoft 12, 22, 42, 65, 67, 189, 209
developers 36
diversifying 87-89

equity 11, 13, 19, 25, 104
expos and trade shows 34-35

financial advisers 22, 26

gazumping 96
goods and services tax (GST) 217

How to Create an Income for Life 2, 5, 12, 22, 47, 101, 102, 113, 115, 124, 167, 174, 181, 190
How to Make Your Money Last as Long as You Do 47, 123, 174
How to Maximise Your Property Portfolio 41, 116, 119, 166, 167, 190, 200, 220

interest-only loans 113-115
interest rates 11, 116-117
internet 31-33, 39, 61, 91, 155, 219

Jenman, Neil 37
joint name purchases 102-103, 190-193

landlord's insurance 217
landlord's responsibilities 166-167
land tax 67, 145, 178, 193
land titles office 66
lawyers 142-143
leaseback agreements 75, 160-161
lines of credit 114, 115

Index

lenders 16
— choosing a lender 123, 136-137
— discharge fees 66
— lender's mortgage insurance 11
— loan to valuation ratio (LVR) 118
— valuers 16
loan applications
— acceptable income 119
— approval rate 21
— documents 121, 126
— establishment fees 66
— fixed rates 116-117
— lending criteria 17-22
— Mortgage Loan Application Checklist 130-134
— prepaying interest and expenses 194
— principal and interest 113-115
— procedure 120-122
— security 118
— submitting 124
— tax implications 112-113
— timeframe for completing 122
— variable rates 116-117
location, choosing 29-30

negative cash flow 25
negative gearing 3-5, 7
negotiations 94-95
newspapers 32

ongoing costs 67-68, 83
on-paper deductions 7-9, 46, 48, 174, 180-186
on-site management 50
open house inspections 208

population growth 70
positive cash flow property 7-9, 25
— calculations 53-54
positive gearing 5-6
property booms 89-90
property clubs 33-34
property managers 74, 154
— choosing a manager 168-170
— costs 158-159, 171
— fees 67
— leaseback agreements 75, 160-161
— management agreements 163-165
— residential property 154-159
— terminating services 159, 163, 165-166
Property Portfolio File 2, 41, 104, 127, 174, 198
purchasing costs 65-67, 81-82

quantity surveyors 42, 183
— fees 67, 178
— report 174

real estate agents 37-38
real estate institute 39-40, 69, 84, 92

record keeping 194-195
rental guarantee 73
rental property schedule 179, 183
renting 218-219
requisitions on title 145
research 40-41
revenue costs 177-179
risk profile 52, 56-60

safety margins 17
selling
—agent 205
—agreements 206-207
—costs 209, 211-212
—process 204-209
—reasons for 200
seminars 218
serviced apartments 50-51

settlement 147-148
—settlement agents 142
stamp duty 65, 146-147, 176
strata titled property 46, 145
structuring your purchase 102-103, 190-193

tax returns 173-174
—deductions 4, 17, 22, 117, 154, 182
terminating management services 159, 163, 165-166
title search 66, 143

vacancy rates 69
vacant land 50
valuations 127
valuer general 193-194
variable rate loans 116-117

DESTINY FINANCIAL SOLUTIONS

Destiny Financial Solutions can assist you with a range of investment needs, as follows:

1. Investment workshops and seminars

Margaret Lomas frequently conducts evening seminars and national workshops. The aim of the seminars is to provide clarity on information contained in Margaret's books and to allow attendees the chance to have their personal questions answered.

The workshops will be a full day format at which investing in general will be discussed. This will assist all investors to make wiser choices about their investing future. Attendees will receive a workshop manual and an investor pack. To express your interest in attending either a workshop or a seminar, phone 1800 648 640 or email us at:

workshop@edestiny.com.au

Watch the website for more information about all Destiny events.

2. Personal support and assistance

Destiny Financial Solutions is expanding its network to provide personal assistance by trained branch staff in many areas throughout Australia. We can assist you to put together a personalised property investing strategy which is not reliant on the purchase of a particular property. All of our branches offer financial advising support and assistance for direct property investors. Phone or email us, or visit the website to find out our branch locations or to ask about the unique services we can offer.

3. Free download

Phone 1800 648 640 or for email instructions contact:

download@edestiny.com.au

4. Join the Destiny team

Exciting business opportunities exist for enthusiastic people to join Margaret's team. Visit the website for more information on these opportunities.

Thank you for reading this book. We can be contacted at:

info@edestiny.com.au

For assistance with your finance needs contact:

finance@edestiny.com.au

For download instructions, contact:

download@edestiny.com.au

If you would like to tell us how you felt about this book, or make a suggestion for future books, please contact:

margaret.lomas@edestiny.com.au

Destiny Financial Solutions Pty Ltd
PO Box 5400
Chittaway Bay NSW 2261
Ph: 1800 648 640
www.edestiny.com.au